Ouija Board

A Mare in a Million

Ouija Board

A Mare in a Million

Lord Derby

highdown

RACING POST

Published in 2007 by Highdown
an imprint of Raceform Ltd
Compton, Newbury, Berkshire, RG20 6NL

A catalogue record for this book is available from the British Library.

ISBN 978-1-905156-40-5

Designed by Adrian Morrish

Printed by Butler and Tanner

Frontispiece: Oujia Board (Kieren Fallon) greeted by her owner after winning
the 2004 Breeders' Cup Filly and Mare Turf
at Lone Star Park, Texas

CONTENTS

Epsom Reclaimed

Dim the lights, set the scene, call the spirits home,
Dunlop's brought the filly forth, the one that runs alone.
Tighten belts, letters spell names of heroes past,
Demons of the track are here, punters' eyes aghast.
Fingers on the glass are firm, set for shock 'n' awe,
Kieren's pressed the button now – what's she got in store?

'I'll tell you what she's got,' said one, 'of what she's got in store,
'Just wait and see, just stick around, behold the ghosts of yore.
'You'll see the power of Shergar when he bolted down the hill;
'You'll see Nijinsky's footwork as he steadied for the kill.
'You'll hear The Minstrel's war cry when the battle reared its head,
'A Sea Bird's flash of brilliance when he left his field for dead.
'And if, like you, her jockey looks to her and asks for more,
'You'll see Secreto dash the hopes of swift El Gran Senor.'

So how is it that centuries on, the famous Black and White
Have found a horse that once again returns them to the site
Where famed 12th Earl of Derby gave renown to Epsom Downs,
And set the scene for noble beasts to run for racing crowns?
The 19th Earl, Lord Edward, did your ancestors conspire
To return you to this hallowed ground, re-spark the family fire?
Did you sit around a table? Did you slowly dim the lights?
Did the blood of those who'd gone before demand you stand and fight?
And in honour of this setting, where the spectral crowds still roared,
Was it then you had to leave a clue, and name her Ouija Board?

Dim the lights, set the scene, call the spirits home,
Dunlop's brought the filly forth, the one that runs alone.
Fingers on the glass are firm, set for shock 'n' awe,
Kieren's pressed the button now – what's she got in store?

She's opened up the gunnels, she's dealt a crushing blow,
She's left them toiling in her wake, she's brushed aside the foe.
She's given back to England, she's brought us home the Oaks,
She's broken up a stranglehold and given people hope,
That at this place atop the hill, it's not part of a hoard
For gents from Ireland and Dubai – bring on the Ouija Board.

And if one day in future years, as darkness claims the sun,
You stand alone on Epsom Downs and dream of victories won,
You might just hear her challenging for one last great success,
Battling bravely for the line with Meld and Sun Princess.

HENRY BIRTLES

PREFACE
OAKS DAY, 2004

When the bell rings, the signal for jockeys to mount, I feel the pit in my stomach deepen with nerves and anticipation. Ed Dunlop gives the final riding instructions to Kieren Fallon as travelling head lad Robin Trevor-Jones helps our jockey spring into the saddle.

Once Kieren has mounted, Ouija Board continues to walk round the

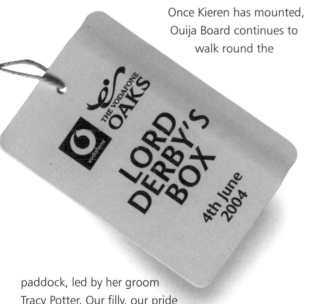

paddock, led by her groom Tracy Potter. Our filly, our pride and joy, looks a picture as she starts to make her way out to the racecourse. The paddock at Epsom Downs is, as always before a Classic race, brimming with horses, connections, officials and the media. This is my first ever runner in a Group 1 race and this race is the Oaks, the Classic named after my forebear's house at Epsom.

My throat is dry with nerves. I have just finished being interviewed by Clare Balding for BBC television, and have said how exciting a prospect it is for the famous Derby colours – black, white cap and a lucky white button – to have a chance of winning the first Classic for the family since Watling Street's wartime Derby in 1942, and how I feel the omens might be with us since my Aunt Bridget is in the paddock with us that day and the 12th Earl of Derby had won the inaugural running of the Oaks in 1779 with a filly named ... Bridget.

The tension is broken only by the inevitable wisecracks from Willie Carson, whose great career in the saddle had started as the Stanley House jockey for my uncle, the late 18th Earl of Derby.

My wife Cazzy and I join the jostle of people leaving the paddock, returning to the stands to have a bet or watch the horses go down. Too nervous to wait for the lift, we rush up the four floors by the emergency stairs to get to the box we rent for the Derby meeting every year, and watch the field of seven beautiful fillies parade in front of the Grandstand.

Our girl looks fabulous. All the team have done all they can to get her here; now it is down to her, Kieren, the opposition and the fates to decide what will happen next.

After the parade, the fillies canter gently around the course, up the hill and down the back straight, to the start. They circle behind the starting stalls, waiting for the starter to signal that it is time to start loading. They are probably only circling for a minute or two, but it feels like an eternity.

Finally the gates open and a huge cheer rises up from the crowd.

Ouija Board comes out of the stalls fairly slowly, which is intentional as we do not want her to have too prominent a position early on. It is a small field and a white cap is always easy to spot, and that familiar cap remains in a steady position towards the rear as the horses go up the long haul towards the top of Tattenham Hill, then sweep left-handed and come down the hill towards Tattenham Corner.

Round the corner and into the straight come the runners. Prize money will be paid down to sixth place, so beating just one horse home means that I will be able to say that I have won prize money in an English Classic. But no, better than that, the team is doing well, sweeping on, moving forward. I have no eyes for any other horse. I merely see Ouija Board working her way past the colours of both Sheikh Mohammed's Godolphin and the various Magnier colours, travelling sweetly and continuing to work her way through the field.

We are going to be placed ... no, even better – she is going to be second! Then, after the two-furlong pole she hits the front, and the noise around us of everybody screaming and cheering is deafening. Will another runner come and catch her? ... No – she is comfortably at the front ... Kieren is showing her the whip but has no need to strike her, so well is she going.

One length clear, then two and three, and still she comes on. Four lengths, five, six – and at the line she is seven lengths clear of her six rivals. I feel myself being lifted skyward in a euphoric state – and then it is hugs, kisses and screams all round, all a blur as we charge back down the staircase and rush out onto the course to go and congratulate our heroine, Kieren, and Ed and Becky Dunlop, who have watched separate from us at ground level.

By the time we get to Ouija Board, a furlong beyond the finish, Ed, Becky, Robin and Tracy are already there with her. But the ecstasy is with us all. Tracy leads her on the near side, while I join Robin on the off side, glowing with pride as I guide this wonderful filly back to the cheering crowd and huge throng of press and photographers that has collected on the course.

Seeing your colours come past the winning post in first position is always a wonderful feeling, but for them to be such historic colours in a Classic – and one with such a close family connection – just magnifies the whole experience. After a very happy pause for photographs we lead Ouija Board into the famous Epsom winner's circle.

How the omens have come good for us. We have all been wearing the same outfits on Oaks day as we had for her most recent victory in the Pretty Polly Stakes at Newmarket a month earlier on One Thousand Guineas Day. We will surely stick with these lucky outfits through all her career.

Clare Balding introduces the formalities; Cazzy, Ed, Kieren and myself all mount the winner's rostrum to be presented with trophies by Arun Sarin, chief executive of Vodafone, sponsors of the Oaks, and I raise the beautiful trophy, a galloping horse in silver, for all to see and share in my unadulterated happiness. The Epsom executive lead us all – fifteen, twenty, perhaps twenty-five of us, I have no idea exactly how many – into the press room to watch a re-run of the race and to celebrate our victory with champagne and talk joyfully of our happiness and future plans ...

The 2004 Oaks started an extraordinary journey that over the next three years led us many times around the world with our amazing, our wonderful Ouija Board. This is her – and our – story.

CHAPTER ONE

'AN AWFUL LOT OF CLASS'
OUIJA BOARD'S EARLY YEARS

The story of Ouija Board is the story of how a large group of individuals – stud staff, trainer and stable staff, vets, farriers, jockeys, work riders, flying grooms and numerous others, and yes, the owner as well – bring together their individual skills to make a champion racehorse. Her extraordinary success was the result of a massive team effort, though the first members of that team could hardly have been aware of what they were initiating when they delivered a dark bay filly with a small white star on her forehead at the Stanley House Stud in Newmarket on 6 March 2001.

It was in the box immediately adjacent to the stud office, where foals belonging to the current Lord Derby are traditionally born, that the filly foal by Cape Cross out of Selection Board was brought into the world at 11.25 a.m. by Pat Cronin, stud groom at Stanley House for a quarter of a century, and my brother Peter Stanley, who manages the stud.

Pat remembers the delivery of the filly foal by Cape Cross as perfectly straightforward and uneventful – which, since she was the tenth foal of her dam, was only to be expected – and within the hour the foal was standing to suck milk from her mother. (See foaling record on page 204.)

For my brother Peter, the foal was 'nice, but nothing remarkable', while Pat Cronin, who has delivered thousands of foals in his time, remembers the filly as having 'a wonderful conformation'. When my wife Cazzy and I first

Left: Edward Smith Stanley, 12th Earl of Derby (1752-1834), by George Romney, c.1782.

met the newcomer a few days later, we thought her lovely to behold, but nothing out of the ordinary. She was very well

made, but at that point there could be no hint of the qualities which would make her the most globally popular of any horse in my family's long racing history.

That history has made 'Derby' arguably the most resonant word in world racing, but there had been eleven Earls of Derby before my ancestor the 12th Earl gave his name to the most famous race in the world.

The title dates back to the fifteenth century. In 1482 Sir Thomas Stanley, 2nd Lord Stanley, married Lady Margaret Beaufort, widowed mother of Henry Tudor. In 1485 Lord Stanley helped secure the throne for Henry at the Battle of Bosworth Field – final battle of the Wars of the Roses – and was rewarded by Henry VII (as Henry Tudor had become) with the title Earl of Derby, which name refers not to the county of Derbyshire but to the hundred of West Derby in Lancashire, where Knowsley Hall had been the home of the Stanleys since 1385, and remains the family seat.

So began the Derby line, which has been closely connected with the progress of English history. The 2nd Earl, grandson of the first, was with Henry VIII during the French expedition of 1513; the 3rd Earl, who inherited at the age of twelve, was famous for his liberality; the 4th Earl and his son Ferdinando, Lord Strange (who became 5th Earl) and William, the 6th Earl, had a company of players which employed William Shakespeare; the 7th Earl sponsored a horse race – the original Derby – on the Isle of Man, where he was Lord of the Island, and was beheaded for his loyalty to Charles I; later in the seventeenth century, the 9th Earl preferred the country to the

Court and was the first Earl of Derby to show a significant interest in horse racing; and Edward Smith Stanley, the 12th Earl, was as significant a figure as any in the annals of the Turf.

One of the most familiar stories in racing history is how in 1779 the 12th Earl – who had been born in 1752, the year that the Jockey Club was founded – inaugurated a new race on Epsom Downs, named after his house nearby: The Oaks. (The Earl kept a pack of staghounds which hunted the country around the Downs, and *The Earl of Derby's Staghounds* was a famous painting by Sartorius – prints of which, by remarkable coincidence, were to be found adorning the walls of our hotel room in Louisville, Kentucky, in November 2006.)

The Oaks was the second of the races we now know as the Classics, three years younger than the St Leger, which was first run at Doncaster in 1776, and it represented a further move away from the traditional manner of running races in heats, with a run-off determining the winner. Like the St Leger, the Oaks was a 'Stakes': that is, each owner put in a specified sum of money, and after a single contest rather than heats the prize fund was awarded to the winner.

The inaugural Oaks, run over a mile and a half up on the Downs, was won by the Earl's own filly Bridget, and at a dinner to celebrate his victory – when the guests reportedly included such luminaries as General Johnny Burgoyne (fresh from the American War of Independence), and the politician Charles James Fox. Also present was Sir Charles Bunbury, one of the great racing administrators of the eighteenth century, and the

fable goes that when a new race was proposed for the following year – this time a race for colts as well as fillies – it was agreed that Bunbury and Derby should toss a coin to determine whose name the race would bear. Sadly there is no document in the archives at Knowsley Hall to confirm or deny this familiar tale, but whatever its veracity, it was as the Derby Stakes that what was to become the most famous horse race in the world was run on 4 May 1780, over one mile. (The present distance of 1½ miles was first used in 1784.) The Earl himself won the eighth running in 1787 with his colt Sir Peter Teazle, named after a character in the play *A School for Scandal* by Richard Brinsley Sheridan, who reputedly had been another of the guests at the famous dinner party when the race was born.

Eventually 'Derby' would be commandeered into the title of hundreds of horse races around the world – familiar ones like the Kentucky Derby, and less familiar like the Kiplingcotes Derby, run over open country in Yorkshire – and the word spread outside racing to a Donkey Derby, the British Jumping Derby, and any number of football games between neighbouring teams: thus Liverpool versus Everton is popularly called the 'Merseyside Derby'.

Racing colours had originally been registered not long before the first Derby and Oaks, in 1762, and while the Earl of Derby's colours were not in the first officially published list, they were originally registered as 'green with white stripe[s]'. But the same colours were registered by Lord Foley, and in 1782 also by Lord Egremont, and so as to avoid confusion in 1788

Right: Peter Stanley with the Edward Seago portrait of Hyperion.

the 12th Earl changed the family colours to the famous 'black, white cap', which have been the Derby colours ever since – except that, as we shall see, the modern colours feature an unregistered white button.

The 12th Earl, who was Lord Lieutenant of Lancashire for fifty-eight years, died in 1834 at the age of eighty-two and was succeeded by his son Edward, a noted zoologist who established a menagerie at Knowsley Hall which included 94 species of mammal and 345 species of bird. Edward Lear was brought in to paint the animals, and during his time at Knowsley entertained the Earl's grandchildren with verses and limericks: Lear's *Book of Nonsense*, published in 1846, is dedicated to those grandchildren.

When the 13th Earl died, the menagerie was

Detail of The Earl of Derby's Sir Peter Teazle beating Lord Clermont's Bullfinch, Newmarket 1787 *by J. N. Sartorius – showing the original Derby colours of green and white stripes.*

dispersed under the terms of his will, much of it going to Queen Victoria, some to the Royal Zoological Society at Regent's Park in London (which formed the basis of what is now London Zoo), and the rest through public auction.

The talents of the 14th Earl lay in other areas: he served as Prime Minister three times (1852, 1858-9 and 1866-8), and was also a noted scholar and poet as well as maintaining a keen interest in racing: while he never won the Derby itself, his horses amassed over £100,000 in prize money, an enormous sum for those days. His son the 15th Earl, who as Lord Stanley won the 1851 Oaks with Iris, devoted most of his life to politics, and has the distinction of serving in the Cabinet as a Tory and later as a Liberal. The 16th Earl, Frederick, became Governor General of Canada in the late 1880s: he founded the Stanley Cup, still the major trophy in Canada's national sport, ice hockey. After his return to England on succeeding to the title he devoted much energy to founding the Stanley House Stud in Newmarket to complement the existing stud at Knowsley, and twice owned the Oaks winner: Canterbury Pilgrim in 1896 and Keystone II in 1906.

In developing the family studs – which were later expanded to include the Plantation and Side Hill Studs at Newmarket and the Thornton Stud in Yorkshire – the 16th Earl was closely assisted by his son, Edward George Villiers, my great-grandfather, who as 17th Earl was much loved locally and affectionately known as 'The King of Lancashire'. Born in 1865, he had a distinguished political career, including serving as

Derby Has Added Glamour This Year
* * * * *
rd Derby, for Whose Ancestor the Course at Far-Famed Epsom Downs was
Named in 1783, Will Attend This Year

CHURCHILL DOWNS
KENTUCKY

EARL of
DERBY

EPSOM DOWNS
ENGLAND

ropriately enough, this year's
-ky Derby winner will be
ed with the cup of victory
Earl of Derby, illustrious
a statesman and sportsman.
English peer from whose
the great race and the derby
eived their names, has just
t New York by his flat re-
o be lionized.
sixty-four-year-old Earl,
as served his country as
ry for War under three
Ministers and also as Am-
or to France, is making his
sit to the United States in
ears.
in New York harbor by Po-
ommissioner Grover Whalen
e Committee for the Recep-
f Distinguished Visitors, the
diplomat said he was here
to see the Kentucky Derby
have "seventeen days of
ood time."

Lord Derby, a jovial, florid-
faced man weighing more than 200
pounds, entered New York carrying an umbrella, although there
was a cloudless sky. His friends
explained that it was a lifetime
habit of his, as he lives in Liverpool, a city that suffers from almost daily rainfall.
"I know I shall be caricatured
during my visit," he laughingly
told ship news reporters. "But
please let me say this: I do not
wear a monocle or spats. I do
not carry a cane and I smoked my
last cigar forty-five years ago.
"When I present the cup to the
winer of the Kentucky Derby I
will plead with my hearers to pro-
nounce the name of the race darby.
After all, you know, my family
was its godfather."
The Earl declined to discuss the

naval parley, the English unem-
ployment situation or other national and international problems.
His views on these important matters will be reserved for the series
of banquets American notables are
giving in his honor.
The Earl produced final proof
that he possessed a sense of humor
when asked which was the best
run derby he ever saw.
"The finest derby I ever witnessed," he declared, "was the one
I won myself. The next finest
was the one in which I backed the
winner at fifty to one."
At Churchill Downs, where the
American turf classic will be run
on May 17, Lord Derby will be the
guest of Joseph E. Widener, mil-
lionaire racing enthusiast of Phil-
adelphia.
After the race the Earl will
hurry back to England for the
English Derby at Epsom Downs.

How the Evening News of Paterson, New Jersey, reported the 17th Earl's visit to Kentucky in May 1930. By a happy coincidence, the photographs connect the venues of Ouija Board's first and last Group 1 successes: Epsom Downs, where she won the Oaks in June 2004, and Churchill Downs, where she won the Breeders' Cup Filly and Mare Turf in November 2006.

Secretary of State for War during the First World War, after which he became Ambassador to France.

His influence on racing and breeding in the twentieth century was immense: indeed, so immense that when *Racing Post* journalists John Randall and Tony Morris produced their book *A Century of Champions*, Lord Derby was allotted the number 1 slot in the section 'Makers of Twentieth-Century Racing'. The introduction to his entry sums up why:

Lord Derby won a record number of Classics as both owner and breeder, and his status as the most influential figure in twentieth-century racing can be summed up by the statement that, without the stallions and broodmares that he bred, the modern Thoroughbred as we know it would not exist.

Swynford, Phalaris, Pharos, Colorado, Fairway, Hyperion and Alycidon were among the champions bred by the Derby studs who became outstanding sires, and their descendants and those of many other Derby stallions and broodmares became cornerstones of top-class breeding throughout the world.

The 17th Earl of Derby won the race named after his great-great-grandfather three times: with Sansovino in 1924, with the great Hyperion (who also won the St Leger) in 1933, and with Watling Street in 1942, when the Derby was run not at Epsom but at Newmarket's July Course on account of the war. His stallions headed the list of champion sires in thirteen of the twenty-four seasons from 1923.

One of the old racing scrapbooks which has been preserved at Knowsley includes extensive cuttings about the visit which the Earl made to Kentucky in 1930 to watch the Kentucky Derby at Churchill Downs. He was feted as if royalty, declined to offer a tip for the big race – 'There's many a man in London will tell you I've made a lot of people bankrupt with my racing tips' – and was asked about the future of international racing, which had become an issue of interest seven years earlier when Papyrus, winner of the Derby at Epsom, had made the long journey to Belmont Park in New York for a match race against the American champion Zev. In sloppy conditions which put Papyrus at a severe disadvantage on the dirt track, the American horse won easily, and the venture was considered something of a disaster by the connections of Papyrus. The Earl of Derby commented:

You know, I never saw racing over a dirt course before Kentucky Derby Day last Saturday. One can't compare racing here with that in England because of the difference between courses. I think there is no course – and by this I mean the racing strip – in all the world like the turf at Newmarket.

Nor can you compare horses here with those at home, because they cannot run against each other. The thought of running our best here or your best in England is ridiculous.

Sending Papyrus over here was one of the stupidest things I ever heard of. Do you think I would send a good horse over here for a race? The idea is perfectly ridiculous! I would not add to the fame of my horse by winning over here,

but I certainly would jeopardize it. And so would any American who sent a horse to England.

Even if you did have one of those international races, you never would get the best horses from abroad. Their owners at home would not send them.

These comments take on a particular significance in the light of the international feats achieved by a horse carrying the Derby colours over seventy years later!

When the 17th Earl died in 1948, having outlived two of his three children, he was succeeded by his grandson and my uncle John, who had been born in 1918 and had been awarded the Military Cross during the Second World War for his efforts at the battle of Anzio in Italy. In 1971 he founded Knowsley Safari Park, thereby restoring the tradition of having exotic animals on the estate, and maintained the family tradition of a strong interest in racing and breeding, though on a scale smaller than had been pursued by the 17th Earl. In 1949, the year after he succeeded, the 18th Earl started to reap the harvest sown by his predecessor, with Swallow Tail being beaten by two heads in the Derby and then winning the King Edward VII Stakes at Royal Ascot, and the great stayer Alycidon going through the season unbeaten, his five victories including the Ascot Gold Cup, Goodwood Cup and Doncaster Cup, the 'Stayers' Triple Crown'.

The 18th Earl's finest horse in later years was the hugely popular gelding Teleprompter, whose exploits are recent enough to be familiar to most present-day racing enthusiasts. His biggest wins came in the Queen Elizabeth II Stakes at Ascot in 1984 and the immensely valuable Budweiser Arlington Million the following year – and to mark that famous victory in Chicago a rhino calf born at Knowsley on the day of the race was naturally christened Budweiser!

Teleprompter has a particularly honoured place in racing history as a horse who prompted a change in the rules. Before Teleprompter geldings were ineligible to run in Group 1 races in Britain, but he was so good that to deny his participation at the highest level was clearly a nonsense, and in 1986 that rule was amended, though geldings are still not allowed to run in the Classics. Naturally Teleprompter could not make a contribution to the Derby blood lines, and

Teleprompter, ridden by Tony Ives, winning the 1985 Arlington Million from Greinton.

it is fair to say that after the heady successes of the racing and breeding operation under the 17th Earl, the fortunes of the stud went into some decline under my uncle the 18th – not least because he was loath to weed out from the breeding stock those mares who were not producing progeny of sufficient quality.

Teleprompter ran his last race in 1987, having won eleven races and nearly £800,000 in prize money – then a record for a European-trained gelding – and after spending some time at the family's Woodland Stud in Newmarket was taken to Knowsley. Cazzy had put in a call to Teleprompter's trainer Bill Watts to ask for pointers about riding him, and had been told: 'Whatever you do, don't take him out of a canter, or you won't be able to hold him – Willie Carson never could! And he's used to being the lead

horse, so always be in front.' One way and another, not an ideal hack, but none the less Cazzy rode him around the estate until, soon after he had arrived, she discovered that she was pregnant with our first child Henrietta.

Teleprompter played a major part in developing my own interest in horse racing. With the Turf so deeply embedded in our family's history, it is hardly surprising that from my earliest years I was aware of the sport, though my brother Peter, two years younger than myself, was always much more knowledgeable, and passionate about racing to the point of obsession. The family connection with the sport was further strengthened by my mother Rosie Spiegelberg being the daughter of trainer Nan Birch (who as Nan Kennedy trained Ra Nova, winner of the prestigious Schweppes Gold Trophy hurdle in 1984) and by my aunt Stella – my mother's sister – being married to the great Irish jockey Tim Molony.

Our holiday home when I was a small child was at Selsey in Sussex, from where Peter and I would go to Fontwell Park and Goodwood, and a day at the Epsom spring meeting, in the box which my uncle shared with The Duke of Devonshire, was the customary end-of-holiday treat before returning to my prep school Ludgrove: the Duke would provide me with a betting fund of ten shillings (fifty pence after decimal currency was introduced in 1971), which I would spread around two or three horses during the afternoon. (Although betting often adds spice to the racegoing experience, I have had quite enough satisfaction and enjoyment from Ouija Board without ever having had a bet on her.)

When I was seven my father became very ill, and I look back with admiration at how my mother nursed him for two years and saw him constantly in and out of hospital, until he died when I was nine. (My mother later remarried, and it was a great joy to invite her and my stepfather Bill Spiegelberg to Hong Kong in December 2006 to celebrate Bill's seventieth birthday on the very day that Ouija Board would be running her very last race – or, as it turned out, would not be running.)

Peter had always been fanatical about racing, and when we were at Eton our half-term holiday each summer would usually take in a visit to Epsom on Derby Day, spent not in the family's box but up on the Hill, where the unique atmosphere of the occasion could be most thoroughly enjoyed. Another highlight of the year was going to the Grand National at Aintree, where the family had had a box for many years. The first National we saw, but only on television, was the famous 1973 race in which the wonderful Australian chaser Crisp built up such a huge lead that it seemed impossible he would be caught – only for Red Rum to catch him on the line and win by three quarters of a length, in one of the most heart-stopping finishes ever. I have to record that Peter had backed Crisp, and I had backed Red Rum! Since then I have attended almost every Grand National, at first with the family having a picnic at the Canal Turn and in later years joining my uncle in his box.

My mother remembers these days at the races as invariably descending into a battle between Peter's wish to stay for the last race and my anxiety to get back to Eton to row in an eight.

In 1990 Peter and I bought a mare named Sharanella, whom we sent to the stallion Celestial Storm for her first mating. The result was the colt Sonic Boy, whom we sold as a yearling to our old family friend the trainer Fulke Johnson-Houghton for £8,000 and who showed some very decent form, finishing fourth in the Chesham Stakes at Royal Ascot in 1994 (beaten a neck, a head and a neck) and winning three races. Among Sharanella's other offspring was Shuttlingslow – named after a mountain on the Crag Estate where we had grown up – who went into training with Michael Bell and was later moved to Nick Gaselee for a spell racing over hurdles, but never won a race of any sort. My uncle had used the name for a horse many years earlier, so I asked his permission before naming Shuttlingslow: he said it was fine for me to go ahead, but warned me that his horse of the same name had been a very poor performer and was generally known on the racecourse as F***ingslow!

Since those early days I have been trying to breed good horses, always propelled forward by the hope of producing a racehorse better the last one, and I was firmly in the 'useful handicapper' bracket until Ouija Board came along.

On the death of my uncle John in 1994 – when I succeeded, at the age of thirty-two, to become 19th Earl – I inherited, along with Knowsley Hall and Estate, the Crag Hall and Estate on the Cheshire-Derbyshire border and the Stanley House Stud. The complexities and geography of these three estates kept me pretty busy for the next ten years, so I did not manage to go racing as often as I would have liked.

After spending some time in Australia, New Zealand and the USA learning about the bloodstock business, Peter had inherited the New England Stud in 1983 from our uncle Richard Stanley, who had bred the good filly Waterloo, winner of the 1972 One Thousand Guineas in the colours of my aunt Sue, and in 1993 Peter had been asked by our uncle John to become manager of Stanley House Stud/Woodland Stud, in addition to his duties at New England. How lucky I was to be able to call on my younger brother as a wise and knowledgeable stud manager, whose experience and insight were to make him an invaluable player in the Ouija Board team.

When my uncle John had become so ill that we had to start thinking seriously about what would become of the family's breeding interests after his death, Peter and I agreed to meet for dinner in London to discuss the matter. John had said that I should sell Stanley House Stud and keep a few mares with Peter at New England, while Peter was adamant that I should not sell the stud yet. This clearly needed sorting out as a matter of some urgency, but when we met in a London restaurant for the crucial discussion, we were alarmed to find dining at the very next table Nick Assheton, one of our uncle's executors! The conversation we were about to have was clearly not one which Nick should overhear, so we hastily relocated to the Savoy, where Peter persuaded me that with diligent management and carefully controlled costs the Stud could at the very least break even, and even make a small profit. I agreed with him, and how relieved I am now that I did not take my uncle's advice.

None the less, after I had succeeded to the title the necessity to settle death duties led me to sell Stanley House – the house, but not the stud buildings – and some adjacent paddocks to Sheikh Mohammed, who was then beginning to build the Godolphin operation. Sheikh Mohammed had already bought the Stanley House Stables (where he installed John Gosden as trainer) from the trainer Gavin Pritchard-Gordon, who had bought them from my uncle, and when they were renamed Godolphin Stables by the Sheikh we decided to drop the name Woodland Stud and focus on Stanley House Stud, as it was confusing for everyone to have two names in use.

I had my first horse in training while I was at the Royal Agricultural College at Cirencester (where I had started in 1986 after a spell with the Grenadier Guards): Palace Coup, owned jointly with Johnny Strutt (now Lord Rayleigh) and Philip Freedman, later chairman of the Thoroughbred Breeders' Association, whose father Louis Freedman was a prominent owner and breeder whose best horse had been Reference Point, winner of the Derby, King George and St Leger in 1987. Trained at Clarehaven in Newmarket by the late Alec Stewart, Palace Coup brought us a lot of fun but was admittedly pretty useless.

My first winner was Wistful, trained by Michael Bell, in a two-year-old selling race at Leicester in April 1991, and to this day I can still feel the extraordinary rush of adrenalin as I watched my colours – black, white cross-belts, white sleeves, white cap, a theme on the traditional Derby black and white and previously registered by my father Hugh Stanley – pass the winning post in front.

After that I continued to have about two or three horses in training at a time, racing for fun and on a scale extremely modest by the standards of my great-grandfather, and as we looked at that dark bay filly foal at the stud in March 2001 the idea of ever having a horse good enough to win a Classic, let alone a succession of other top races around the world, did not even register on the scale of our dreams.

But this daughter of Selection Board was of special interest from the very beginning on account of her being closely related to Teleprompter, and the story of Ouija Board's breeding in effect begins in 1950.

That year my uncle the 18th Earl, who had inherited the title two years earlier, came to an arrangement with the leading French breeder Elisabeth Couturie – arranged by my uncle's stud manager Colonel Bunty Scrope – whereby, in order to bring new blood into their respective operations, each would give the other one mare. In this way my uncle lost a mare named Amboyna and gained a mare named Gradisca. Amboyna produced Tahiti, winner of the 1952 Prix de Diane, while Gradisca's early matings did not augur well for her influence at the Stanley House Stud. The foal from her first covering in England, by Alycidon, was born dead, and then for two seasons she was barren. In all she produced just two winners, both by Hyperion but neither with much ability.

Alarmingly for a mare whom my uncle hoped would strengthen his broodmare band for generations to come, Gradisca had only two daughters. Almah was such a dismal failure in her first two races that my uncle quickly sold her –

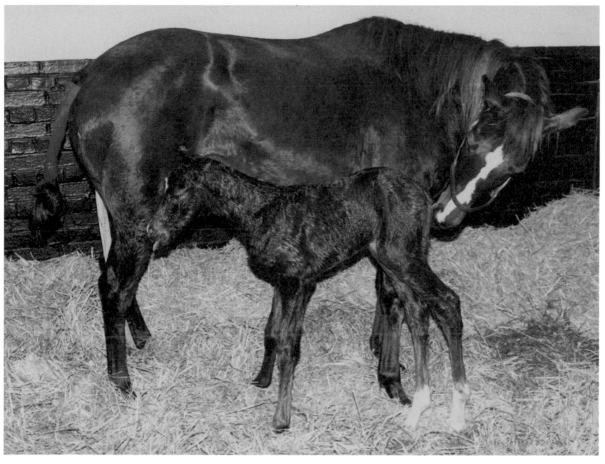

Selection Board, Ouija Board's dam, moments after giving birth in 1991 to her colt foal by Rainbow Quest – who, named Star Selection, went on to win on the Flat, over hurdles and over fences.

and twenty years later her grandson Kingston Town was being feted as one of the greatest of all Australian racehorses.

The other filly was Samanda, a daughter of the great stayer Alycidon, and any potential she might have had seemed to lie in ruins after she had been blinded in a terrible accident as a foal: spooked by some unknown hazard, she panicked and ran full pelt into the rails of her paddock at the Woodland Stud, and her eyesight could not be saved. She was weaned, and to keep her company the stud deployed a pony, to whose head-collar was attached a bell so that Samanda could be aware of where her companion was.

In 1957 Woodland Stud had three stallions – Alycidon, Borealis and the super-sire Hyperion – as well as a full complement of mares, and with the best will in the world it was highly impractical to keep the blind Samanda on the premises: she could not safely be turned out with the other mares, and to have a paddock of her own plus loose box would be an extravagance for a filly with little breeding potential.

The obvious course was to have Samanda put down, but before instructing the stud to do that my uncle contacted Colin Dive, then farm and stud manager at Knowsley, and asked whether they could cope with her at the estate. Colin suggested that Samanda, by then a yearling, and her pony be sent up – 'I felt she was too well bred to be put down and I was sure we could care for her' – and she was duly relocated, and housed in a loose box giving out onto one of the walled paddocks which the 13th Earl had built for his menagerie.

When Samanda was four she was sent off to be mated, returning to Knowsley in foal, and year after year the same process was followed, each new foal being fitted with the bell, which would then be returned to the pony when the foal was weaned. She developed especially acute hearing: Colin Dive, who had effectively saved Samanda's life, remembers how she always had her ears pricked, and she seemed to have little difficulty finding her way around. 'She was a real character,' Colin recalls: 'When you went to her paddock she would charge up to you and then suddenly stop just short of a collision, but once you had a lead rein on her, she was no bother at all.' (While she was at Knowsley, Samanda was regularly shod by Andrew Smith, then an apprentice farrier, and my mother is convinced that the alacrity with which, over the last few years, Andrew has come to shoe her hack reflects his enthusiasm for getting the latest news about Ouija Board!)

Samanda repaid the care lavished on her with twelve foals, of whom ten raced and nine were winners, and one of these was the filly Ouija. Described as a 'big, attractive filly, and a good mover' by Timeform's *Racehorses of 1974*, Ouija did not race at two, but at three proved herself a very good miler, winning at Sandown Park and the Fern Hill Handicap at Ascot before finishing fourth in the Falmouth Stakes at Newmarket.

Having raced for just the one season, Ouija proved highly successful when retired to the paddocks, producing five winners, of whom the best was the result of a mating with the stallion Welsh Pageant: none other than Teleprompter, the gelding who did so much to keep the 'black, white cap' prominent in the mid-1980s. Her other winners included Chatoyant, who won the Brigadier Gerard Stakes, and Rosia Bay, who became the dam of Ibn Bey, trained by Paul Cole to finish second in the 1990 Breeders' Cup Classic, and of Yorkshire Oaks winner Roseate Tern. Unfortunately my uncle had sold Rosia Bay before she showed herself a broodmare of such distinction, and had sold her much against the wishes of his wife, my aunt Isobel, who was mad keen on racing and breeding, and of Peter: between them they tried to persuade my uncle not to sell the mare, but he would not be swayed, and Rosia Bay's departure was, in retrospect, a major loss to the stud.

In 1981, the year after she had produced Teleprompter, Ouija went again to Welsh Pageant, and the outcome was a filly who was to be named Selection Board. Put into training with Bill Watts at Richmond in Yorkshire,

Ouija Board's sire Cape Cross, with Gary Stevens up, after winning the Queen Anne Stakes at Royal Ascot in 1999.

Selection Board ran only twice. She came second in a maiden race at Ayr in September 1984 – nine days before her full brother Teleprompter, also trained by Bill Watts, won the Queen Elizabeth II Stakes at Ascot – and at the end of that season Timeform described her as a 'plain, leggy, close-coupled filly' before venturing the opinion that she was likely to improve. But the 1985 season was nearly over by the time she made her second and final racecourse appearance, finishing well down the field in a maiden race at Haydock Park in October. Her career earnings were £832.

By the time in the autumn of 1999 that we started to work out mating plans for the 2000 breeding season, four of Selection Board's offspring had won races. The best of this quartet was Star Selection (by the 1985 Arc winner Rainbow Quest), who ran sixth behind Mister Baileys when a 100-1 outsider for the 1994 Two Thousand Guineas and was twice placed in Listed Races; he won six races in all, one on the Flat, six over hurdles and one steeplechase. His full

Pat Cronin, who brought Ouija Board into the world, outside the box at Stanley House Stud where she was foaled.

brother Spectrometer, whom Selection Board produced in 1997, also ran under both codes and beat Collier Hill (who will reappear in this story) in the Knavesmire Handicap at York in 2002. To his great credit, Peter was always convinced that Selection Board was capable of throwing a Group race winner.

After discussing with Peter, we decided that for her 2000 mating we would send Selection Board to Cape Cross, who stood at Sheikh Mohammed's Kildangan Stud in County Kildare.

Cape Cross had won five of his nineteen races, notably the Group 1 Lockinge Stakes at Newbury in May 1998 (when as a 20-1 outsider he made all the running to rout a high-class field including his Godolphin stablemate Kahal, for whom he was supposed to be acting as pacemaker!), and as a five-year-old in 1999 the Queen Anne Stakes at Royal Ascot and the Goodwood Mile. Never one of the more glamorous horses to carry the royal blue Godolphin silks, he had none the less been a game and consistent racehorse.

Peter had always been keen on Cape Cross as a stallion prospect, so keen that towards the end of the horse's racing career he had attempted to buy the son of Green Desert, to stand as a stallion at his New England Stud, where he had stood another son of Green Desert, the 1994 July Cup winner Owington, who had tragically died in 1995 after just one year at stud. The possibility of buying Cape Cross evaporated when it was announced that he would stand at Kildangan Stud, but he still had considerable appeal as a mate for Selection Board. For one thing, he was a strong and imposing stallion with great substance and bone, and several of Selection Board's earlier progeny had, in Peter's words, 'seemed to lack a bit of bone.' And if Cape Cross appealed physically, he also appealed financially, as 2000 would be his first season covering mares. There was no way of knowing how effective he would prove, and consequently he stood at a reasonable fee of €9,000 (about £6,000).

In the spring of 2000 Selection Board travelled to Ireland to be covered by Cape Cross, and after giving birth to her filly foal in March 2001 went to Inchinor, by whom she produced a colt foal in 2002. Unfortunately the colt grew into a very crooked yearling, and when he went to the October Sales in October 2003 we were not expecting him to attract a great deal of interest. But by then Ouija Board was in training with Ed Dunlop, and had run so promisingly in her first race that Ed decided to try to buy her half-brother. He ended up the underbidder, the price of 5,500 guineas at which the yearling colt was knocked down reflecting the colt's poor conformation. Six days later his soon-to-be-famous sister won her first race.

We were never to have the opportunity to produce more siblings for Ouija Board, as Selection Board died in 2002, aged twenty, having in all produced seven winners – though the last of these, Ouija Board, did not win until after her dam had died.

Studying a pedigree on paper is one thing. Witnessing the actual flesh-and-blood outcome of all those careful mating plans in the form of a little foal is quite another. By the time she was about six weeks old, the newcomer was beginning to impress Peter – 'She was showing more quality than Selection Board's previous foals had' – and it was after she was weaned at about six months old and turned out in a paddock with another foal that she began to suggest to Pat Cronin that she might have real potential. 'She had an awful lot of class', Pat recalls. 'Even at that age, you could see from the way she ran round the paddock with the other foal that she had a real change of gear, a kick which the other foal lacked. And she had a wonderful temperament.'

Over the next year the filly grew strong and athletic in the stud paddocks, as the human team around her started to plot her future. For several years it has been the custom of the stud to sell as yearlings the colts we breed and keep the fillies, in the hope that those who perform well on the racecourse will strengthen the broodmare band of the stud in later years, and when towards the end of 2002 it became apparent that only one of our yearlings would be a likely prospect on the racecourse, we had to decide where to send that yearling – soon to be named Ouija Board – to be trained.

Our first connection with the Dunlops, who were to play such a central role in the Ouija Board story, had been made a couple of years earlier, when at the christening in Scotland of Lady Georgina Hope, daughter of the Earl and Countess of Hopetoun, I was a godfather and Ed's wife Becky a godmother. Ed himself had not been present on that occasion, but we met him a little later in the same house, and got on so well that we determined to send a horse to be trained at the wondrously well equipped Gainsborough Stables on Newmarket's Hamilton Road, where he was then retained trainer to Sheikh Maktoum al Maktoum. His arrangement with Sheikh Maktoum allowed him to train a few horses for other owners and he agreed to take our yearling.

Much was later made of the fact that Ouija Board was then my only horse in training, but the truth is that this was simply the consequence of how things had panned out with our 2001 foals.

At about the time when the yearling colts would start to be prepared to go to the sales in the autumn, our filly was prepared in the same way, beginning with the first stages of breaking in.

Pat Cronin had fitted Selection Board's filly foal with a head collar from her earliest hours, and for the first year and a half of her life she had become used to be being led. Then in August 2002, by now a yearling, she was fitted with a bridle, started to grow accustomed to having a bit in her mouth, and was regularly lunged on a long rein, so that when towards the end of that year she was ready to be fully broken she was already comfortable with wearing a bridle and being handled.

To continue her education we sent the Cape Cross filly (as she was known at the stud) to Lemberg Stables at the far end of Newmarket's Hamilton Road, where the next two vital members of the Ouija Board team waited in the form of Eugene Stanford and his wife Jane. Eugene and Jane take in young (and sometimes not so young) horses for breaking in, remedial treatment, preparing for the sales, or rest and recuperation (known as 'spelling'). Eugene is a

highly experienced horseman: he had run the Genesis Green stud near Newmarket for the former royal jockey Harry Carr, and had been with trainer Geoff Toft when one of the inmates of his small Yorkshire stable had been Gunner B, who went on to win the Eclipse Stakes when trained by Henry Cecil. Eugene had later worked as assistant trainer to Mel Brittain and in the USA before joining Newmarket trainer Conrad Allen as assistant.

So our Cape Cross filly was in extremely good hands when she arrived at Eugene's yard in October 2002. His first impression was that she would need a good deal of time to mature before she started racing, which of course was no surprise to us, as we were aware that hers was a late-developing family. Initially she was head-shy, disliking the experience of having a bridle fitted (though she soon got over that) and showed a marked aversion to needles, which with regular blood sampling, vaccination and so on are a routine feature of any racehorse's life. (This aversion never left her.) That apart, the Cape Cross filly was a model of good behaviour, and easily accepted each part of the breaking-in routine.

For her first couple of days she spent regular periods in the horse-walker to help her get used to her new surroundings, and then the breaking-in proper began. She was fitted with a 'breaking bridle', the bit of which incorporates a set of jangly keys with which she would fiddle with her tongue, both to get her more familiar with the sensation of having a bit in her mouth and to toughen up the part of her mouth which the bit would touch.

Then she had boots put on her front legs – again to familiarise herself with what would become a routine sensation – and after a few days was led the short distance from the cosy yard at Lemberg Stables to the daunting wide-open expanse of Newmarket Heath, beside the Rowley Mile. Here she was fitted with a lungeing rein, and for ten minutes each day trotted and cantered round in big circles – switching regularly from clockwise to anti-clockwise direction – to teach her how to respond to the feel of the bit in her mouth, and how to use herself at different paces. Then came a more elaborate system of lungeing reins, with one going straight to the handler and the other going round her far side to replicate the sensation of being ridden with a bit. Some yearlings become very agitated by this sensation, but the Cape Cross filly was as good as gold, as she was the following day when a felt pad with a roller was fitted round her belly.

On the fifth day a racing saddle was placed on her back, and the filly was driven – or 'long-reined' – from the yard to the lungeing ring on the Heath, walking ahead while Eugene guided her from behind. After a couple of weeks of these regular excursions came the build-up to the big moment when the infant horse would accept a human being on her back. In the security of the filly's loose box, Jane Stanford stood at the filly's near side and gently jumped up and down, to get the youngster used to the odd experience of a person suddenly leaping into the air above her. The next day Jane added laying one arm across the filly's back to the jumping up and down, and the day after that – with still no adverse reaction from the well-mannered Cape Cross filly – lay

across her back, and then sat on her. So to Jane Stanford goes the distinction of being the first person ever to have ridden Ouija Board.

For the next two or three days the filly was walked gently round her box with Jane or Eugene in the saddle, and then the education continued outside, with quiet walks around the yard. Before long it was time to take her out onto the Heath, to be ridden in a placid canter for half a mile up one of the nearby gallops, and from then on the routine was repeated practically every day.

Alongside the education in how to run, the young racehorse needs to learn stable manners – how to be amenable in the box – and Eugene was soon struck by how well the Cape Cross filly took to the routine comings and goings into her box. He was struck also by her condition: 'She never grew a winter coat, and if she rolled in her box there was never a scrap of bedding left on her once she'd got herself up. There was a fastidiousness about her. If she'd been a woman she would always have been immaculately turned out.'

During the spring of 2003 Ed Dunlop made regular visits to Lemberg Stables to view the filly. She was considered backward – when Eugene took her out of her box and walked her up and down for Ed, her soon-to-be trainer remarked, 'She's a better specimen stood still' – and when Ed's vet Mike Shepherd, partner at the Newmarket practice Rossdales, examined her, he found her skeletally immature. But there was no hurry to get her into training, and she remained with the Stanfords, routinely enjoying two steady canters each day plus an hour in the horse-walker.

Among the other two-year-olds at Lemberg Stables that spring was a colt later to be named Gravardlax, in whom Peter's wife Frances Stanley had a share, and whom Ouija Board would be meeting again. There were also two youngsters belonging to Sir Thomas Pilkington – who were to race under the names Snow Goose and Woodcracker and who had, coincidentally, been reared at Peter's New England Stud – who regularly went up the gallops with our filly, led by an unraced four-year-old. These canters in the company of other horses were an essential part of our filly's learning curve, and it is interesting to note that both her work companions were to make some mark on the racecourse: Snow Goose was runner-up to Cairns in the Rockfel Stakes at Newmarket, an important late-season race for two-year-old fillies, and won four times, including a Group 3 race in Italy, while Woodcracker won twice, including a valuable handicap at the Newmarket July Meeting in 2004.

By the late spring of 2003 the Cape Cross filly had matured sufficiently to go into serious training, and by now she had a proper name.

Over the last few years, time spent on car journeys – plenty of it in jams on the M6 – has given Cazzy the opportunity to pin me down on matters that need discussing, and one of the most pleasant items on the agenda each autumn has been the naming of our racehorses. The days when a two-year-old could run without being named were long past, and naming our filly could not be rushed as it was always possible that whatever name we wanted – which would be formally registered at Weatherbys, racing's 'civil service' – would already have been taken,

and we would have to think again. One day, stuck in a traffic jam, with me at the wheel and Cazzy with the children in the back, we started to bounce names around for our filly, a process commenced in the traditional manner by considering the names of her sire and dam. Cape Cross out of Selection Board ... Cape Cross ... Selection Board ... the cogs in our brains were working at much greater rate than any in the car's engine, but nothing was striking exactly the right nerve. Then Cazzy said, 'Ouija Board?' – and I turned round to her and exclaimed: 'Brilliant!' Cazzy had not known that Ouija, dam of Teleprompter, was the granddam of the Cape Cross filly, and her making such an inspired and fitting choice was an early omen of good fortune to come. We phoned Weatherbys. The name Ouija Board was free, and was formally registered to our filly. (A ouija board is a device employed at seances for making contact with departed spirits, and in future years the magic connotations of the term were frequently picked up by the press.)

Towards the end of May 2003 the two-year-old Ouija Board made the short journey down the Hamilton Road to Ed Dunlop's yard, which would be her home for the next three and a half years.

Training racehorses is in Ed's blood. His father John, who trains at Arundel in West Sussex, has long been acknowledged as one of the great trainers of the modern age, having won the Derby twice – Shirley Heights in 1978 and Erhaab in 1994 – and handled a succession of top-class horses, including Salsabil, who won the One Thousand Guineas, Oaks and Irish Derby, and the great sprinter Habibti. Ed learned his trade as assistant first to Nicky Henderson at Lambourn and then to Alex Scott, who had been installed as trainer to Sheikh Maktoum at Gainsborough Stables following the untimely death of Olivier Douieb. Ed had no expectation of succeeding Alex Scott at Gainsborough, but was thrust into that situation in the most brutal of circumstances when in the autumn of 1994 Alex was murdered by a former employee at his stud.

Ed took over the reins, though the stable's potential star Lammtarra, whom Alex Scott had trained to win his only race as a two-year-old in August 1994, was moved to the then infant Godolphin operation for a stunning three-year-old career in which he ran only three times, winning the Derby, King George VI and Queen Elizabeth Diamond Stakes and Prix de l'Arc de Triomphe, before retiring unbeaten. It was an extraordinary set of circumstances which had put Ed centre-stage as trainer for one of the world's biggest owners, but the manner in which he and Becky responded won them a host of admirers, and we were delighted to be sending Ouija Board to the yard. Furthermore, Peter had been a very good friend of Ed's elder brother Tim, who was tragically killed in a car crash in France in 1987, and had long been close to Ed himself: they had worked together preparing yearlings at the Stackallan Stud in Ireland.

Ed's view when visiting Ouija Board at Eugene Stanford's yard that she would need time was confirmed when she finally arrived at Gainsborough Stables. He remembers that his first impression of her then was: 'A tall filly; a bit weak; a bit on the leg; nicely made but immature.' His head lad Chris Hinson, who has been working in racing for over forty years and at Gainsborough for nearly two decades – and whose exemplary service was recognised when in January 2007 he was named Stable Employee of the Year at the annual Stable Staff Awards – had no doubt that the new inmate had plenty of promise: 'My first impression was that she had a good bit of class. She was a lovely, big filly, and though she was certainly immature when she first came to us, I always thought she'd become a real racehorse. She had a fantastic temperament, and there was an extra dimension to her. Right from the beginning, she gave me the impression that she'd been in this world before.'

To help her adjust to her new surroundings Chris would take her out each evening for a pick of grass, and she soon settled in, looked after by the first of the three grooms who would tend her during her racing career, Tracy Potter.

The routine of each horse at Ed's stables is logged onto an 'Activity Report' for the entire time he or she is in training, and the first few entries for Ouija Board in late May and June 2003 illustrate how she was quietly introduced to her new life as a racehorse:

> *Friday 30 May*: trotting on the Heath, reached through a quiet walk through the woods
> *Saturday 31 May*: one canter over five furlongs of the all-weather Farm Canter at the back of the yard
> *Monday 2 June*: one canter
> *Thursday 5 June*: one canter
> *Friday 6 June*: one canter

In this way her strength was gradually built up,

Ouija Board – number 21, ridden by Eddie Ahern – finishing third behind Secret Charm (Michael Hills) and Gravardlax (Pat Eddery) in her very first race, the Beech House Maiden Stakes at Newmarket.

but there was no question of her taking part in a race until much later in the season. No exercise was more arduous for the young filly than two canters a day until late August, when she 'worked' – that is, was put through her paces in a formal gallop – for the first time, on the Polytrack all-weather surface alongside the Cambridge Road. In the saddle that day was Steve Nicholson, who the previous year had regularly partnered the then stable star Fraulein in her work. Fraulein had won the valuable and prestigious E. P. Taylor Stakes at Woodbine, Toronto, so when Steve said of Ouija Board after her first work that 'This feels like it could be Fraulein', the stable began to realise that they just might have something special on their hands.

Ed had pronounced himself very pleased with how Ouija Board was progressing, but the real test would be to see her on the racecourse. With her breeding she was never going to be a precocious juvenile and we were well aware that she probably would not show her true ability until she was three, but we were keen to get a race or two into her before the end of her two-year-old season, not least for the experience it would afford her.

It was not until Friday 3 October 2003 that the name Ouija Board first appeared in a racecard, one of a large field of twenty-three maidens – horses who have not won previously – over seven furlongs at Newmarket's Rowley Mile course. (I could not go to Newmarket, but managed to watch the race on television.) The Beech House Stud EBF Maiden Stakes, opening race on the Newmarket programme, was worth £7,137 to the winner but had attracted late-maturing two-year-olds from many of the major stables. Sixteen of the twenty-thee runners were colts, and only six of the field had raced previously, none of them more than once. One of these went off favourite: Mr Tambourine Man, trained by Paul Cole and ridden by Frankie Dettori, who had finished runner-up in another Newmarket maiden race ten days earlier. Second favourite on 5-1 was Gravardlax, in whom my sister-in-law Frances Stanley had a share and who had finished a highly promising fourth in a Newbury maiden – and who a year earlier had been learning his business with Ouija Board at Eugene Stanford's yard.

On the morning of the Newmarket race, the *Racing Post* described Ouija Board thus: 'From a successful but not precocious family; others likely to be sharper at this stage'. Such an assessment was fair enough, as were her predicted odds of 33-1, though in the event she started at 20-1.

We held no great expectations that day and Ed instructed her jockey Eddie Ahern to give her as kindly an introduction to racing as possible. For the first half of the race she was held up, quite close behind the leaders, and then she started to make a forward move, taking the lead with over a furlong to go. But the Barry Hills-trained filly Secret Charm, who was unraced but not unfancied as 11-2 third favourite, and Gravardlax went by her, with Secret Charm running on to win by a neck, with Ouija Board 1¼ lengths further back in third. (Gravardlax, incidentally, never won a race – evidence, were we to need it, of the highs and lows of racing.)

It was a highly satisfactory beginning, and *Raceform* showed characteristic foresight when commenting that Ouija Board had 'shaped with plenty of promise and looks the sort to benefit from middle distances next term.' Those close to the filly at home were more than happy: Chris Hinson thought the race 'a nice introduction'.

The next step was to build on this experience by getting another race into Ouija Board reasonably quickly, and eighteen days later on 21 October she faced just five opponents in the European Breeders' Fund Novice Stakes over seven furlongs at Yarmouth, a contest which in Ed's view would suit her down to the ground, since the small field would be a relatively easy option for our filly

I found this voucher in my overcoat about a year after Ouija Board's first win – by which time it had taken on a special significance!

on only the second race of her life, and Yarmouth is a very fair course on which to educate a young horse.

Since the journey from Knowsley in Merseyside to Yarmouth in Norfolk by road is not exactly easy, and since 21 October is our wedding anniversary, I decided for the first time in my life to charter a helicopter, as Ed was so uncharacteristically confident about her chances.

Our nanny Carole Dowson – an unsung heroine of the team, whose flexibility and devotion to duty made it possible for Cazzy and myself to enjoy the Ouija Board experience to the full – was off that week, so the two elder children Henrietta (then six) and Edward (five) went to my mother's home in Cheshire the day before the race for a sleepover, leaving Oliver, then one and a half, at Knowsley. We flew off – with sufficient champagne and sandwiches to celebrate our anniversary properly – to Yarmouth, where we found Ouija Board in the prime of condition.

We had not been the only ones to have been highly impressed by her Newmarket run, and whereas she had been a 20-1 chance then, this time she started even money favourite, with only Gerard Butler-trained Rydal and Mick Channon's Naaddey

Great Yarmouth
RACECOURSE

Complimentary Owners & Trainers Tea/Coffee & Pastry Voucher

Date of issue
2 1 OCT 2003

To claim please present this voucher to a member of the catering staff in the Owners & Trainers bar

Non-Transferable (non refundable)
Valid only on date of issue

seeming to offer any danger to her getting off the mark.

Ridden by Jamie Spencer, Ouija Board produced a performance which justified the helicopter hire and, more to the point, showed us that we had a serious racehorse on our hands. *Raceform* noted how Ouija Board 'conjured up a sweet performance' and predicted that 'There could be some nice prizes to be won with her next season over further [distances],' while the *Racing Post* reporter at Yarmouth that day had picked up on the double significance of the day for the winning owner:

Ouija Board made sure that her owner Lord Derby's wedding anniversary went with a swing when an impressive winner of the seven-furlong novice stakes.

The even-money shot showed signs of greenness when racing in behind in the early stages and hung left when hitting the front over a furlong out under Jamie Spencer, but the magic was certainly there as she showed an impressive burst of speed to scoot four lengths clear of Rydal to earn a 40-1 quote from William Hill for the 1,000 Guineas.

I do hope that anyone considering taking William Hill's generous 40-1 for the 2004 One Thousand Guineas managed to hold themselves in check, as there had never been any intention of entering her for that race, which would have come far too early in the season for her. In any case, at this stage we were not entertaining any lofty aspirations for her whatsoever. It was very much a question of taking one step at a time, and when

Ouija win puts Lord Derby in mood to celebrate anniversary

OUIJA BOARD made sure that her owner Lord Derby's wedding anniversary went with a swing when an impressive winner of the seven-furlong novice stakes.

The even-money shot showed signs of greenness when racing in behind in the early stages and hung left when hitting the front over a furlong out under Jamie Spencer, but the magic was certainly there as she showed an impressive burst of speed to scoot four lengths clear of Rydal to earn a 40-1 quote from William Hill for the 1,000 Guineas.

The daughter of Cape Cross had shown plenty of promise on her debut at Newmarket 18 days earlier and her trainer Ed Dunlop said: "She is a nice filly and the first I've had for Lord Derby.

"He came all the way down from Liverpool on his wedding anniversary and I'm glad the journey was worthwhile.

"The family shouldn't be d much at two and she is by C Cross, who as we know has pleasant start to his stud ca

"She will be given some s entries and we'll see how sh over the winter."

Her first headline – in the Racing Post, *22 October 2003.*

Ed pronounced himself 'happy but not ecstatic' over her performance, that was good enough for us, and we took the helicopter back to Knowsley – stopping off *en route* to land on the motor racing circuit at Oulton Park, right by my mother's house, to pick up Henrietta and Edward – in a very happy frame of mind.

Yarmouth may not be the most glamorous racecourse, but I was delighted by her wide-margin victory, and especially pleased as she was the first two-year-old winner I had ever owned.

Ouija Board came out of the race so well that we decided to give her one more outing in 2003 – the more experience a two-year-old can get, the better equipped he or she will be for the following season – and on 1 November she returned to Newmarket for the EBF Montrose Fillies Stakes over one mile. This was a Listed Race – the level below Group races, so a reasonably high-class contest – and in addition to Ouija Board's stepping up in the grade of race she was stepping up in trip, the mile being a furlong further than she had previously contested. There

was another factor which, with the future in mind, made this race an important step in our fact-finding mission. Her first two races had been on going officially designated good to firm, while for her third the ground was good to soft.

Ouija Board's Yarmouth win had impressed all who saw it, and we were not surprised that, despite the fact that she was now meeting opposition of significantly better quality, she again started favourite, at 11-4. Her principal rival in the market was Spotlight, who had run second in the Oh So Sharp Stakes at Newmarket – another Listed Race – in early October, and before

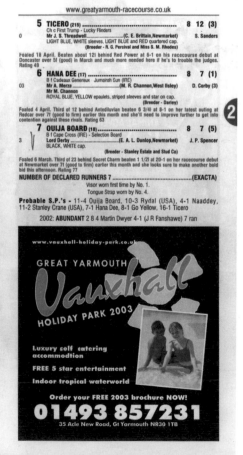

that had won a maiden race at Warwick; she was trained by Ed's father John Dunlop.

Ridden again by Jamie Spencer, Ouija Board was slowly out of the stalls, and with Spotlight taking an immediate lead and running on powerfully, was never able to get in a blow. Through the final furlong she kept up the chase and looked sure to finish runner-up, then right on the line was caught by St Francis Wood and beaten a short head for second. Spotlight, who was eleven-times champion jockey Pat Eddery's final winner in Britain, was a comfortable four-length winner.

Ouija Board had been beaten, but an important consideration was that, since the Montrose Stakes was a Listed Race, she had got her 'black type'. When a sales catalogue gives the racing record of a mare and her progeny, a win or placing in a Group or Listed race is printed in bold type to advertise its status, and thus the amount of 'black type' in an entry proclaims the overall quality of that pedigree. Even if Ouija Board were never to win another race, getting that black type would be an important consideration when, if ever, it came to selling her offspring. In addition to rightly being thrilled that she had got her black type, Peter was convinced that if this member of a late-maturing family could boast a two-year-old record of one win and two thirds, she was a surefire Stakes winner for the following year.

A few days after her last race of the season, Ouija Board returned to Stanley House Stud for the winter, to relax after the more rigorous atmosphere of the training yard. Weather permitting, she would be turned out in a paddock for four or five hours each day, and Pat Cronin did a superb job in keeping her in the peak of condition.

But there was sadness for the family that autumn, for Teleprompter, who was then rising twenty-four years old and had enjoyed a contented retirement under Peter's watchful eye at the stud, was beginning to go downhill quite rapidly and causing us a good deal of concern. Then in October the stallion Inchinor, who stood at Stanley House Stud and was the sire of Ouija Board's final sibling, died following an operation to mend a fractured pastern. He was only thirteen years old and was proving a highly dependable stallion, so his loss was a shattering blow. In the circumstances we decided to get all of our sadness out of the way at once, and after a good deal of soul-searching had Teleprompter put down before the ravages of winter made him even more miserable.

With the gloom behind us we could then concentrate on the future. Ouija Board, our only horse in training, had enjoyed a highly respectable two-year-old career, and we were well aware that whatever she did as juvenile, she was always going to improve as she got older.

We had plenty to dream about over the months ahead.

CHAPTER TWO

'THE PEOPLE'S FILLY'

THE 2004 SEASON

After spending most of November and December at Stanley House Stud, Ouija Board returned to Gainsborough Stables to start rebuilding her fitness towards the time when she would be ready to race, while the team started to focus more on the issue of what should be her first main target for the year. Although we fervently hoped she would prove good enough to compete against the top horses at Group level, we were realistic enough to know that such a course could not be taken for granted. As the cliché goes, it was a question of taking every race as it comes, but such was the esteem in which our trainer held her that he had been considering the 2004 Vodafone Oaks a serious possibility, and when that race closed in early March her name was duly among the entries. We had not known in advance that Ed was planning to enter her, but the fact that he did so underlined his great expectations for the filly, and his opinion that in order to be better than average she needed to stay.

Although there was plenty of speed in her pedigree, Ed and his staff knew that the key to Ouija Board was to teach her how to settle, and thus conserve her energy to help her get distances of a mile and a quarter or longer. Head lad Chris Hinson started to ride her in all her work from the beginning of her three-year-old career, and concentrated on teaching her to relax when cantering in behind other horses of her own age, talking to her as they went up the gallops as a way of encouraging her to switch off. One canter a day was increased to two, and Chris's careful tutoring was soon paying off.

Sheikh Maktoum's investment in Gainsborough Stables ensured that the yard has long enjoyed state-of-the-art facilities. The equine swimming pool allows horses to be exercised without putting undue strain on the body, so vital for those who have suffered the strains and knocks which are routine occupational hazards for racehorses, as well as providing a welcome complement to the regular exercise of trotting, cantering and galloping. The ice water spa, which maintains a constant temperature of minus 3 degrees Centigrade, is likewise invaluable for aiding the recovery of strains and other leg injuries – Ouija Board was to find this particularly beneficial later in her career. At the other end of the heat spectrum there is a solarium in which horses can be warmed through with infra-red heat lamps, a sort of equine sunbed often deployed by the internationally-minded Ed Dunlop operation to start the acclimatisation process for horses about to leave the bracing Newmarket air for the warmer climes of Dubai or Hong Kong. The yard has its own fully equipped forge, and a veterinary unit complete with a sophisticated computer system which allows the medical details of each horse to be instantly updated.

Ouija Board had spent the first period of her working life in the range of boxes which houses the stable's two-year-old fillies – fillies and colts are segregated in the yard – then on her return for her three-year-old campaign was moved to one of the huge barns which form three sides of Gainsborough's main yard, and here she came into the care of barn manager Steve Young.

She could not have been in better hands. Steve has been at Gainsborough Stables since the time of Oliver Douieb and was now effectively second head man to Chris Hinson, and his contribution to settling Ouija Board in the stable routine and preserving intact the equable temperament which so many had already noted in her was a crucial element in making her the horse she became.

Ouija Board's daily routine during her three-year-old career was soon established: Steve Young arrived at the yard at 4.30 a.m.; checked that Ouija Board (and the other two dozen horses in his barn at this point) was safe and sound; put the first feed of the day into her manger; took and recorded her temperature; and left her to finish her breakfast in peace. Later in the morning, while she was out for her daily exercise, he put her second feed of the day in her manger to await her return, and when she came back in he washed down her legs, checked for any grazes or cuts, and put her box bandages and her rug back on. She was then left alone until about 3 p.m., when Steve returned to take her temperature again and feel her legs – any problems to be reported to Ed when he comes round for evening stables – and, from about 5.30 p.m., give her another feed.

While the afternoon feed usually consisted of a bowl of naked oats, the composition of the other daily feeds would vary according to where Ouija Board was in her training programme – for example, whether she was in full work or recovering after a race. For a horse running on the Flat, the summer feeds will concentrate on high energy elements, and Ouija Board's standard feed during her time in training would be a mixture – prepared to Ed's particular specifications – of bran, molasses, glucose and oats, plus small feed pellets. In the winter a lower-octane 'working cube' was sufficient.

When the weather was clement she was led out for a pick of grass, and variations from the routine included being trotted round the yard's vast indoor school, which houses a small set of starting stalls: being made familiar and comfortable with the stalls is an essential part of a young horse's education, and the inmates of Gainsborough Stables are taught from their early days that stalls hold no terrors.

While Steve Young gives the same amount of care and attention to every horse in his charge, he always had a soft spot for Ouija Board – 'She was a joy' – and recognised early that there was something special about her: indeed, something so special that before she had run as a three year old he backed her for the Oaks at 40-1.

Just how wise an investment this was would become much clearer after she had run for the first time as a three-year-old, and Ed had identified the Swinley Stakes at Ascot, a one-mile Listed race for three-year-old fillies at the end of April, as a possible starting point for the campaign. Jamie Spencer, who had won on Ouija Board at Yarmouth, was now based in Ireland as retained jockey for the Coolmore operation, and Ed approached Frankie Dettori about riding her at Ascot. Frankie went and rode work on her, afterwards pronouncing her 'a really nice filly, maybe Group 3 or 2, maybe even Group 1', but then the rains came, producing the sort of soft ground which we knew she would not like, and the Ascot plan was abandoned.

Instead we turned our sights on the Pretty

Polly Stakes, run at Newmarket's Rowley Mile course on the same day as the One Thousand Guineas, four days after the proposed Ascot race. But with Frankie likely to be claimed to ride for Godolphin in the Pretty Polly we needed an alternative jockey, and were fortunate to secure the services of Kieren Fallon, who had then been champion jockey five times. His principal retainer was with the powerful stable of Sir Michael Stoute, who did not have a runner in the Newmarket race, and a couple of days before the meeting he came to ride second lot on Ouija Board – and reported that she was in a different class from Sir Michael's likely Oaks filly whom he had ridden earlier that day.

By the time of the Pretty Polly Stakes, fifth race on the Sunday programme, Newmarket was already buzzing with the outcome of the One Thousand Guineas, in which Guy, Duke of Roxburghe's filly Attraction, whose forelegs had been so bad as a yearling that she had looked an unlikely sales prospect, and whose ungainly but effective galloping action had conformation experts scratching their heads, had beaten Sundrop half a length after making all the running. Secret Charm, who had won Ouija Board's first race, finished a highly respectable fifth, which added fuel to our optimism.

In a field of nine for the Pretty Polly, Ouija Board started 2-1 favourite. The pick of the opposition appeared to be Opera Comique, from Sheikh Mohammed's Godolphin camp and ridden by Frankie, and Aidan O'Brien's Kisses For Me, ridden by Johnny Murtagh.

Approaching the final

The Pretty Polly Stakes: Ouija Board and Kieren Fallon scoot home.

quarter of a mile Kieren, who had held Ouija Board up in the rear for most of the race, still seemed in no hurry to move her closer to the leaders, and Cazzy, watching the race with Peter and me in the stand, was very concerned that she was so near the back. I told her not to worry – and as if he had heard that comment, Kieren exerted a little more pressure on the accelerator, and before we knew it Ouija Board was in front.

Having gone into the lead with more than a furlong to go, she might have been expected to have to withstand a challenge from behind. Instead she went further and further clear, and without Kieren having to ask her a serious question passed the post six lengths ahead of Sahool.

This was an astonishing moment, for we suddenly realised that we had not just a very good horse, but a really top-class one. All things were now possible (and Peter, ever quick-thinking, rushed off to increase our insurance cover on Ouija Board!), but hard on the heels of the excitement came the realisation that we would have to think long and hard about her future programme. This was no longer a case of having fun with a better-than-average horse; it was a case of taking every step to ensure that a very good horse was campaigned to achieve the very best she could. (Ed, for one, had had a sense of how good she could be. When, shortly before the Pretty Polly, Sheikh Maktoum had been taken round the yard, the trainer had had no hesitation in taking his employer to Ouija Board's box and proudly introducing the Sheikh to 'my best three-year-old.')

The Prix de Diane over 1 mile 2½ furlongs at Chantilly was a strong possibility for her next outing, but in the immediate aftermath of the Pretty Polly the press assumed that Ouija Board would be aimed at the Oaks at Epsom Downs on 4 June, nine days earlier than the French race. Under the headline 'OUIJA BOARD SENDS RIGHT SIGNALS FOR EPSOM', the *Racing Post* described her Pretty Polly victory as 'breathtaking', and continued:

Just as the ink was drying on the new Oaks book following the Guineas, the Ed Dunlop-trained filly's victory made them reach for the Tipp-Ex with a quite awesome display ...

Ouija Board was generally third favourite for the Oaks, but with Coral was as low as 8-1 second favourite behind Sundrop, whose odds had contracted sharply following her good run behind Attraction.

As for which race she would be aimed at, Ed told the press: 'She could go for either the French or English Oaks. There is a doubt about her pedigree [i.e. whether she would stay the 1½ miles at Epsom] but there is only one Oaks.'

Scarcely had Ouija Board been led off towards the Newmarket washdown boxes than the big debate within the team started: should she go to Epsom on the first Friday of June for the Oaks, second oldest of the English Classics, a race which my family had founded way back in the eighteenth century, and was run over 1½ miles; or should she go for the Prix de Diane at Chantilly nine days later, the French equivalent of the Oaks but run over a furlong and half shorter?

There were very strong arguments on both

sides, and none of us was 100 per cent for or against.

My brother Peter was especially torn. On the one hand, it had been a fervent ambition of his all his working life for our family stud to breed an Oaks winner, for he knew that were we to achieve that we could indulge the dream of rebuilding the Derby bloodstock operation towards its former glories. On the other hand, his breeding expertise and instinct was telling him that Ouija Board might have trouble staying the mile and a half of the Oaks, whereas the Prix de Diane was more or less the same distance as the Pretty Polly Stakes, in which she had routed the opposition. There was solid evidence to support Peter's reservations about our filly's stamina: Teleprompter, the most distinguished member of the family, was essentially a miler, though in Peter's view his optimum trip was nine furlongs; and Ouija Board's sire Cape Cross had shown his best form at a mile and never ran beyond nine furlongs. Shunning the idea of letting his heart rule his head, Peter came out strongly for the Prix de Diane.

Weighing against Peter on the question of stamina was the fact that in the Newmarket winner's enclosure Kieren Fallon had said to Cazzy that Ouija Board would have no trouble getting the Oaks trip – and Kieren, more than any of us, was in a position to know. Cazzy's conviction that we should go to Epsom was further underlined by the enthusiasm shown for Ouija Board by Lord Vestey's wife Cece, who had become a great fan of our filly after seeing her race as a two-year-old, and had told us in January that we had a Classic winner on our hands. While

we were agonising after the Pretty Polly, a postcard arrived from Cece:

If Ouija Board were mine – would that she were – I would definitely run her in the Oaks. Only once in a lifetime do you maybe own a filly like that. The Pretty Polly is 1 mile 2 furlongs and she won by six lengths staying on. OK, Cape Cross was a miler but in his dam's pedigree (Park Appeal) is Shadayid, who won the One Thousand Guineas and was third in the Oaks ...

In the opposite camp was Philip Freedman, who sent Cazzy a page from the magazine *European Breeding Digest* in which the breeding expert James Underwood explained the reasons why, in his opinion, Ouija Board would not stay twelve furlongs.

Ed, convinced that she would stay the trip, was very keen indeed to run her in the Oaks. He had not yet trained the winner of an English Classic and knew that in Ouija Board he had, as he put it, 'my first proper shout', but in the end the final decision had to be mine. One moment I thought the Prix de Diane the sensible option – we knew she'd stay the distance, and Chantilly is a far less eccentric course than Epsom – and the next concluded that it had to be the Oaks, the race which had been founded by my ancestor. After all manner of soul-searching the decision was made and the long run of sleepless nights at last came to an end. The Oaks it would be.

Family history played a major part in our reaching that conclusion – in addition to founding the race, my ancestor the 12th Earl had owned the inaugural winner Bridget, and several members of the family had won the race since – but there was also, beside the niggling doubt about Ouija Board's stamina, the practical consideration that the Prix de Diane was later. During the two weeks in which we were weighing the options, Ouija Board was in blooming good health: the Newmarket race had taken little out of her, and she was working very well on the gallops. What if we decided to go to France, and close to race day she scoped badly and had to be withdrawn? Then we would have regretted not taking our chance at Epsom. And if some minor hiccough prevented her running in the Oaks, there would still be the Diane to go for.

In a sense Ouija Board made the decision for us. Two weekends after the Pretty Polly she galloped on the Polytrack and worked so well with her usual lead horse False Promise – 'Sensational', as Ed recalls it – that she seemed to be telling us that her next race could not come soon enough.

A week or so before the Oaks I had lunch with Jim McGrath, BBC racing commentator and 'Hotspur' on the *Daily Telegraph*, and Geoff Lester, newly appointed President of the Horserace Writers' and Photographers' Association, of which I am Patron and which stages, at its annual awards lunch in early December, the only event I attend that begins with champagne at 11.45 a.m. and gets a fresh wind when the cash bar opens at 4.30 p.m.! I was amused to read this in Geoff's column in the *Racing Post* the following week:

And stand by for an Oaks fairytale ... Having just been appointed President of the Horserace Writers' and Photographers' Association, I had lunch for the first time last week with our patron Lord Derby, who owns Ouija Board. What odds the 19th Earl being Owner of the Year at our lunch in December if she wins?

Superstition has always played a part in the lives of most racing people, not least the Earls of Derby across the centuries. If you look carefully at the silks worn by jockeys riding in the Derby colours, you will notice that the time-honoured description 'black, white cap' does not tell the whole story. One button – the second button from the top – is always white, and deliberately so, a curious feature which dates back to Tommy Weston riding Sansovino for the 17th Earl in the 1924 Derby, the jockey's first ever ride in the race. Weston was so nervous when donning his silks in the changing room before the race that he inadvertently wrapped his white stock around the second button down before doing his jacket up. Sansovino duly won, and photographs of my great-grandfather leading the horse in clearly show the white button. So struck was the 17th Earl by this little incident that thereafter his colours always incorporated the lucky white button, and the Derby colours do so to this day. (It is amusing to see whether due account is taken of the white button when the Derby colours are reproduced in racecards or signage at racecourses. I noticed that in Hong Kong the white button has been allowed for, but that the programme for the Derby Awards lunch of the Horserace Writers' and Photographers' Association does not!)

Continuing the family tradition of

Ladies in green: left to right, Perina, Lady Braybrooke, Bridget Hanbury and Tabitha Lillingston.

superstition, Cazzy and I agreed that for the Oaks we would wear the same clothes as we had on the day of the Pretty Polly Stakes: that is to say, I would wear the same suit, shirt, tie and shoes as at Newmarket, and Cazzy would wear the same navy blue outfit with a new hat. To make even more certain of placating the racing gods, Ed and his wife Becky likewise wore the same outfits as they had at Newmarket.

Getting so het up about what we were going to wear on Oaks day suggests a high level of tension in the Ouija Board camp, but the fact is that, having made the big decision to go to Epsom and not Chantilly, on the approach to the race itself we were reasonably relaxed, a mood assisted by the sight, on entering our box at the racecourse, of three of our party – my stepmother-in-law Perina, Lady Braybrooke, my aunt Bridget (a wonderfully propitious name for the Derby party on Oaks day!) Hanbury and Tabitha Lillingston, wife of Irish breeder Luke – quite coincidentally wearing outfits of identical lime green. Thus was a new superstition born after the success of Ouija Board later that afternoon.

As so often in the build-up to a big race these days, most of the press attention focused on runners from the two major racing operations of British racing, Godolphin, the brainchild of Sheikh Mohammed, and the Tipperary-based Coolmore Stud, whose horses were trained by Aidan O'Brien. Lord Derby and his only horse in training was little more than an enchanting sidebar to the race coverage, and I was more than happy not to be in the limelight. As the Queen's racing adviser John Warren had said to me in a taxi on the way to the Derby Club Dinner, which traditionally takes place at the Savoy Hotel a few days before the race itself, 'Third favourite means you have an odds-on chance of being placed', and Guy Roxburghe, whose wonderful filly Attraction had put him in a similar position to us and who had joined us in the same taxi, concurred: 'Just enjoy it while it's there.'

Coolmore and Godolphin certainly merited the bulk of pre-Oaks coverage, as between them they were responsible for five of the seven runners in the Classic. Coolmore saddled All Too Beautiful, who started 11-4 favourite and who last time out had won a Listed Race at Navan. Godolphin had the 3-1 second favourite Sundrop, who had run so well when runner-up in the One Thousand Guineas, and also third favourite Punctilious, winner of the Musidora Stakes at York: at a starting price of 100-30 she was marginally preferred in the betting to Ouija Board, who started at 7-2. The other three runners were Necklace (10-1) and Kisses For Me

(66-1) from Coolmore, and Crystal (25-1), trained by Brian Meehan.

For us there was no pressure, and with prize money for the Oaks going down to sixth place, we had only to beat one home for me to collect prize money in an English Classic – which illustrated my level of expectation, and which my mother said would pay for Cazzy's hat.

We were again able to secure the services of Kieren Fallon, as Sir Michael Stoute, who at the time had first claim on his services, did not have a runner in the race, and waiting for the runners to load, it struck me how right all the omens were. It was 225 years ago that the 12th Earl of Derby had inaugurated the first running of the Oaks – a race which, like its brother the Derby, has been replicated right around the world – and seen the first running won by his filly Bridget, and my aunt Bridget was now in our party for Oaks day. It was 100 years since the brilliant Pretty Polly had won the Oaks, and Ouija Board had won the race named after that iconic filly at Newmarket – and the 2004 running saw the joint-smallest field since Pretty Polly's year. If ever I was going to see a Classic won in my colours, it was now.

Through the race I only had eyes for Ouija Board, and with such a small field it was easy to keep track of Kieren's white cap. As before, she was slow out of the stalls, but this was intentional, as we did not want her to have too prominent a position early on. All the way to the top of Tattenham Hill that cap remained towards the rear of the field, then as the runners came down the helter-skelter towards Tattenham Corner it started to move towards the head of affairs – and then when they straightened for

Ouija Board wins the Vodafone Oaks from All Too Beautiful – what a margin she has put between herself and the fancied runners from Coolmore and Godolphin on the big screen! – and the conquering heroine is greeted by Team Ouija.

Ouija Board poses with her proud owner — and I cannot believe how many photographers wanted to record the moment. I particularly loved this photograph when it was published in the Racing Post as it includes a host of family members there to share this very special moment, but it has an extra significance: Sheikh Mohammed, a true lover of horses, can be seen on the right of the picture coming to admire a great horse, even though she is not his own.

Ouija Board and Kieren Fallon led into the winner's circle by Tracy Potter – who had had her hair permed before the race and was asked by Ouija Board's grateful owner to repeat that operation before the Irish Oaks. Thus was born yet another superstition.

home the amazing truth started to envelop me. She was going so easily that she was sure to be placed! – no, better, she'll finish second! – and then, near the two-furlong pole, she hit the front, and my world exploded like a firework display. Even if something now came and caught her, she'd run a fantastic race – but instead the very opposite occurred. Kieren shook her up and she simply took off, like a wave surging over rocks, and as she went further and further ahead – four lengths, five lengths – I had the strangest sensation of being lifted into the air, as pandemonium exploded around me in the box. (In my naivety it had not occurred to me that the BBC would have a camera focused on us all jumping up and down like a bunch of idiots!) Six lengths clear, seven – and then she was flashing past the winning post. Not only had Ouija Board won the Oaks; she had won it in scintillating, breathtaking, astonishing style. I had never before tasted such pure, unsullied, 100-per-cent-proof joy.

The rest of Oaks day 2004 was, I have to admit, something of a blur. I made no attempt to usurp Ouija Board's lass Tracy Potter from leading our heroine into the winner's circle – Tracy lived with her every day at home, and fully deserved the moment of glory – so I walked in at the other side of the filly's head. I remember John Magnier, the driving force behind the phenomenally successful Coolmore operation, and Sheikh Mohammed being among the first to congratulate me; I remember waves of good will enveloping us from every side; and I remember being completely unable to rein in my euphoria during the press, television and radio interviews after the race.

A Derby victory in the Oaks was an achievement which needed celebrating in some style, but finding a table for eighteen in a London restaurant on a Friday evening at a couple of hours' notice proved rather difficult, so I called Fizzy Barclay, wife of Aidan, owner of the Ritz. The Barclays worked wonders in accommodating our party and generously provided champagne on our arrival – and were even able to set up a video machine in the Marie Antoinette Room where we could watch a recording of the race, kindly couriered from Epsom courtesy of Jim McGrath and my second cousin Clare Balding, who had been covering the race for the BBC.

The other big Ouija Board party that evening was up in Newmarket. As we were getting ready to go out, Ed and Becky were enduring a very slow journey home, taking the full brunt of Friday evening on the M25. After arriving home they

Watching the Oaks again at the Ritz. My sister-in-law Frances Stanley and Cazzy are in the front row, with behind them (left to right) my stepfather Bill Spiegelberg, Lucy Manners, Christopher Hanbury, Julia Delves-Broughton, David Beamish and Louise Hatch.

were able to join a large number of the Gainsborough Stables staff in The Yard – a pub frequented by many Newmarket stable staff – where I had put some money behind the bar. A recording of Ed's first English Classic triumph was shown over and over, and then they moved on to The Fountain, their favourite Chinese restaurant, where over the next two and a half years plenty of other Ouija Board victories would be celebrated.

In the days following the Oaks we were bombarded with cards, letters, faxes and emails of congratulation – my mother had a letter from an old friend whom she hadn't seen for forty years – and I was especially taken with a letter from Sir Mark Prescott, who for many years had trained a horse or two to race in the Derby colours, and who recently had handled Ouija Board's older siblings Coalition and Spectrometer:

My Lord,

I am writing this brief, illegible and inadequate note of congratulations (after evening stables on the evening of the Oaks) on the basis that by now your fax machine will have run out of paper. If it hasn't, it should have done so!

What a wonderful day for you, the stud, Peter and 'Young Ed' it must have been; but also, what a great day it was for the sport of racing to see those legendary colours winning a Classic at Epsom – their spiritual home – again. It quite restores my faith in a merciful God!

Having been brought up collecting cigarette cards of Lord Derby horses, having been weaned reading Tommy Weston's autobiography and grown up devouring George Lambton's Men and Horses I Have Known*, I can remember glowing with pride when the late Lord Derby first sent me a horse to train.*

How I wish that by now I could have trained you a Classic winner, but how greatly I enjoyed Ed's great triumph for you – albeit vicariously!

Having trained two out of the dam of Ouija Board, I did feel that the filly was likely to get the trip, and how pleased I was (for once) to be proved right and how I savoured the moment Fallon tucked her in again three furlongs out, as she was going so well. What a sight to treasure. I expect you will never forget it!

May you all have more wonderful days to come with the filly, but whatever happens the big one is already in the bag.

Another letter came from former trainer Gerry Blum: 'Having served my apprenticeship at Stanley House during the reign of the 17th Earl of Derby and having looked after four Classic winners, it certainly brings back happy memories of the good old times.' And Dick Francis wrote that he had toasted Ouija Board's success at a restaurant near his home in the Cayman Islands: 'I know the Derby colours have been highly successful in the Classics for generations past – even I well remember Hyperion's Derby win back in 1933 – but I think yesterday's win was the first in your own name, wasn't it? And may it be the first of many more to come.'

We enjoyed the press reaction to Ouija Board's victory. Following the triumph of Guy Roxburghe's filly Attraction in the One Thousand Guineas and the Irish One Thousand Guineas (which she won by a length from Alexander Goldrun, of whom we will be hearing more) and of the recently deceased Duke of Devonshire in the Irish Two Thousand Guineas with Bachelor Duke, certain journalists took great glee in declaring 2004 the racing year when the old aristocracy had fought back against the new powers in racing. Of course, there was a very limited amount of truth in this – I had just one horse in training, while the combined ranks of horses owned by the Maktoum family and by Coolmore would run into thousands – but it was all meant, and taken, in good part.

The *Sun* headlined its Oaks report with 'BOARD OAKS IS ANOTHER FOR TOFFS', and began, 'Good Lord! Racing's toffs are staging a

Classic revolution.' The *Racing Post* deployed the word magic again in the headline 'RIVALS DAZZLED BY OUIJA MAGIC' and also stressed the theme of the old aristocracy:

The aristocracy is back in racing, and how, as the Oaks was restored to its founders yesterday.
The old order was confirmed the new order when Ouija Board claimed the famous prize for the 19th Earl of Derby, 225 years after the 12th Earl had captured the first running of the Classic with Bridget.

The day after the Oaks, North Light won the Derby for Ballymacoll Stud, under whose auspices horses bred by the late Lord Weinstock and his son Simon (who died tragically young) were

raced, and we liked the piece by the always highly amusing Alastair Down in the *Post* the following week:

You may have heard Peter Reynolds of Ballymacoll Stud talk about Arnold and Simon Weinstock being 'ruthless' in weeding out the chaff from their broodmare band; well, hats off to Teddy Derby and his brother Peter, who have weeded their whole shebang down to one horse in training who wins the Oaks. Now that's what I call being selective.

When we were able to gather our thoughts as the immediate excitement subsided, I took great satisfaction from the knowledge that Ouija Board was the ninth filly owned by a member of the family to win the great race founded by the 12th Earl. For the record, the nine are:

1779	Bridget (12th Earl)
1794	Hermione (12th Earl)
1851	Iris (15th Earl, as Lord Stanley)
1896	Canterbury Pilgrim (16th Earl)
1906	Keystone II (16th Earl)
1928	Toboggan (17th Earl)
1935	Quashed (Lord Stanley, son of 17th Earl)
1945	Sun Stream (17th Earl)
2004	Ouija Board (19th Earl)

The owner gets his name in the record books and banks the prize money, but winning any horse race, big or small, is always a team effort, and we were keen to celebrate Ouija Board's Oaks win with those who were not able to be there on the

Ouija Board and Kieren Fallon on the Cambridge Road Polytrack before the Irish Oaks, with the Millennium Grandstand of the Rowley Mile in the background.

day but had played such a crucial part in her success: the staff at the Stanley House Stud where she had been born and reared and at Gainsborough Stables, where she had learned her trade so well from Ed and his team, and where she was now the most distinguished resident.

On Sunday 20 June we put on a party at Gainsborough Stables, complete with a balloon sculpture shaped like a jockey's silks (in the Derby racing colours of black and white and with the white button), a barbecue, specially produced Ouija Board baseball caps, a South American band – the lot. About 150 of Ed's and my stud staff and pensioners were there, with spouses and partners, Ouija Board was paraded, and it was wonderful to sense the mood of celebration spreading out across the whole operation which had made her the horse she was. We decided to have a similar party at Knowsley in August.

Meanwhile there was her next race to consider.

Ouija Board's winning the Oaks considerably raised our sights, and the obvious next race for her was the Irish Oaks at The Curragh on Sunday 18 July. She had not been entered for the race at the original entry stage – such was our initial reluctance to consider that she might be anything out of the ordinary – but the £150,000 she had earned us from her winning the Oaks meant that we did not have to ruminate for more than about two nanoseconds about whether to pay the €30,000 to supplement her into the race, and have the chance to go for dual Classic glory.

Ten days before the Irish Oaks, Kieren Fallon, who would be riding her at The Curragh, worked her over a mile on the Cambridge Road Polytrack

– one of only two pieces of work she had between the Oaks and the Irish race – and pronounced himself well satisfied, and when ante-post betting started in earnest she was installed as 4-5 favourite to become the tenth filly to win at Epsom and then follow up in the Irish equivalent.

Apart from Punctilious, who after running third behind Ouija Board in the Oaks had won the Ribblesdale Stakes at Royal Ascot, there was no other English-based runner in the Irish Oaks, and since Punctilious was from Godolphin and therefore had use of that

Before setting off from Spain for The Curragh, with our friend Richard Burrell and our wonderful flight attendant, whom we nicknamed 'Dolores'.

organisation's private transport, we were faced with the extreme expense of sending our one horse to The Curragh. So Ed suggested that Ouija Board should be accompanied by her lead horse False Promise, whose presence would help her relax on her first overseas trip.

Unfortunately the Irish Oaks clashed with a family holiday in Spain which we had booked long before we had any intimation that Ouija Board's commitments would put any strain on our diary, and we were adamant that we would not deny the children their time away. But nor could we bear to miss Ouija Board's race at The Curragh, for adding the Irish Oaks to the Epsom original would take her to yet another level of excellence, and prove that her Oaks performance would in no way be a fluke.

Cazzy and I investigated the logistics of making a day trip from southern Spain to Ireland by scheduled flights but the timings did not work out, so in another rare moment of extravagance we decided to charter a private plane to take us from Marbella to Dublin in the morning and back to Marbella after racing: the children would remain in Spain in the excellent care of their devoted nanny Carole. Early on the Sunday morning we were welcomed aboard the five-seater jet by an impossibly good-looking stewardess, and – accompanied by our friend Richard Burrell, whose family were with us in Spain – flown in the lap of luxury to Dublin airport, where a car whisked us to The Curragh in good time.

There was more tension before the Irish race than there had been at Epsom, one indication of which was our deploying an extra guard to be stationed outside Ouija Board's box at the racecourse stables. She was odds-on favourite for a Classic, and security was an issue.

Winning the Oaks had put Ouija Board conclusively at the head of her generation and sex, and from being a possible winner at Epsom she was now elevated to the status of expected winner: owning the odds-on favourite in a Classic really builds up the pressure. Was her run there a freak? Had Epsom been a dream?

One highly important point that the Oaks win had made was that Cazzy and I had been entirely justified in indulging our superstition and wearing the same clothes as on the day of the Pretty Polly Stakes, and there was not the remotest possibility of ourselves or Ed and Becky wearing anything else at The Curragh. But the increasing tension on the drive to the Curragh from the airport meant that we had to harness every possible good omen to retain even a semblance of calm, and we started to fret about whether we would see another lime green outfit: the profusion of lime green in our box on Oaks Day had been a harbinger of a famous success, and it was important to know that the colour was properly represented for the Irish Oaks. Mercifully, the first friend we saw on arrival at the course was Luke Lillingston's mother Lady Vivienne wearing the same lime green that her daughter-in-law and others wore at Epsom. I took this as a lucky omen and started to relax a little – and was delighted that Peter and Frances and their ten-year-old son Hugh, along with my mother and stepfather, had flow from England to join the Dunlops, Cazzy and I. We were entertained to lunch at

The Irish Oaks: Ouija Board goes clear of Punctilious.

the Turf Club by Jonathan Irwin, one of the towering figures of the Irish bloodstock business and the brains behind the founding of the Goffs Million, the earliest version of the vastly valuable sales races which are now a feature of the racing year.

In the Irish Oaks, as at Epsom, there were seven runners, including the first three in the Oaks, whose Epsom finishing order was reflected in the betting. Support for Ouija Board had hardened as the race approached and she went off 4-7 favourite, with All Too Beautiful on 4-1 and Punctilious 5-1.

Ouija Board's performance completely justified the effort we had made to be there. Yet again slowly away from the stalls, she settled in about fifth position for the first mile, making headway entering the straight. As that point she did not appear to be going as smoothly as at a similar stage at Epsom, and Kieren was pushing away – but she responded by taking the lead a furlong and a half out and stayed on strongly to go clear, then near the finish was eased to pass

*Ed and Becky Dunlop
savour the moment.*

Back at the Marbella Club, celebrating Ouija Board's victory at The Curragh on the Monday evening. The Racing Post headline on the day of the Irish Oaks, asking 'IS THERE ANYONE OUT THERE?', was followed on the day after by the headline 'QUESTIONS ANSWERED'.

showed the tension which we were all were feeling: it was such a relief to be able to watch it once all that nervousness had been replaced by the joy of another great victory by our filly.

I managed to get hold of a *Racing Post*, in which the previous morning's headline 'IS THERE ANYONE OUT THERE?' – that is, any filly to rival Ouija Board – was given the Monday-morning reply, 'QUESTIONS ANSWERED'. (After our return Chris Smith, editor of the *Post*, kindly sent me a high-quality copy of both front pages to frame.) The Monday edition carried an engaging piece by Peter Thomas:

There are notices posted all round the racecourse announcing that smoking is now prohibited at The Curragh. Clearly nobody had informed Ouija Board, who flouted the law by leaving a trail of exhaust for her outclassed rivals to splutter on as she scorched to a second Classic success.

the post a length ahead of Punctilious. While at Epsom I had had that extraordinary sensation of leaving the ground with elation, this time I felt my knees buckling with sheer relief. This was not a dream, but reality. If not as spectacular as Epsom, it was a comprehensive victory, one meriting a generous plaudit from Kieren: 'She's unbelievable, the way she switches off and then accelerates.'

Unbelievable she certainly was, and for us the Ouija Board story was getting more incredible with each succeeding race. We flew back to Spain that Sunday evening completely shattered but elated, and celebrated the following day over lunch with the children and the Burrells, filling the Irish Oaks trophy with champagne with which we toasted our heroine. Richard had brought a video camera with him to The Curragh, and his video diary of our day in County Kildare clearly

And while the stragglers were still catching their breath, the lofty Ed Dunlop, minus ciggy, was breathing a healthy sigh of relief at a satisfactory outcome to what had been a week of unease.

It must be bad enough trying to keep an odds-on Darley Irish Oaks favourite away from the ubiquitous pebble that has been trodden on by so many championship contenders, worse still that the owner has had to stump up €40,000 for the privilege of making the line-up.

Even when you're a toff and you've landed plenty of spondulicks at Epsom, that kind of money isn't trouser change, so it's little wonder that the Ouija Board team had been walking on eggshells.

60

Lord Derby admitted to being the biggest box-walker of the bunch, and paid tribute to his trainer for not only producing his horse in perfect order, but also for keeping the bill-payer from breaking into a muck sweat in the preliminaries.

Opinions varied as to the ease of Ouija Board's success. From the grandstand she appeared to be squeezed along to make up ground on the pace-setting Danelissima before looming large with her challenge.

Even Dunlop seemed surprised to hear Kieren Fallon dismount with the message that the victory had been 'a piece of piss'. The filly had done no more than go to sleep, according to the champion jockey, but when the wake-up call finally reached her, she showed the surge of a champion to sweep past Punctilious.

Whether her failure to press home the advantage in spectacular style was down to renewed drowsiness or fading stamina is open to interpretation, but what is not in doubt is that the connections of the vanquished will have been disheartened to hear Dunlop proclaim that he is itching to drop her back to ten furlongs to draw further improvement from her, and that she will be even better as a four-year-old.

One affable aristo, in the shape of the Duke of Roxburghe, has already cheered racefans this season by mooting the idea of keeping Attraction in training for another year. For Lord Derby to follow suit would be almost too much anticipation for us to bear.

Dunlop wouldn't be upset at the prospect, either. 'I could do with it,' he confided, adding almost unnecessarily: 'I haven't got any better than her at home.'

The owner himself appeared almost sheepish on the subject of having only one horse running for him this year: 'It's the only time in the last decade that I've only had one in training. It's just the way it's worked out. There will be a few more next year and I know which trainer will be getting the pick of them.'

Now we knew we had an exceptionally special filly on our hands, and soon after the Irish race we announced that Ouija Board would stay in training as a four-year-old. After all, when you have one horse and that horse is as good as her, you want to enjoy her as much and for as long as you can. I realised that I was highly unlikely ever to own one remotely as good, and I wanted to enjoy every moment of her career.

Meanwhile there was the matter of the shorter term, and there were numerous options for where she might go next. The King George VI and Queen Elizabeth Diamond Stakes at Ascot was out of the question as it came only six days after The Curragh (though it should be noted that Ed's stable was in flying form at that time, and won the big handicap on King George day with Court Masterpiece, a horse he would transform from handicapper to Group 1-winning miler). Ouija Board had not taken on the boys at the highest level, and the Juddmonte International at York in mid-August was a possibility, but in the end we decided to keep her running against her own sex for the moment and aim her at the Yorkshire Oaks, run on the day after the International on the middle afternoon of York's wonderful Ebor meeting.

With an autumn campaign very much on the

agenda – we were seriously considering the Prix de l'Arc de Triomphe at the beginning of October, and the Breeders' Cup Filly and Mare Turf in Texas seemed to be a race made for Ouija Board – we wanted our filly to have as quiet a spell as possible before York. She had taken a while to get her usually healthy appetite back on returning to Newmarket after the Irish Oaks, and we were learning that she needed time between her races.

Then a week before the race Kieren Fallon, who would ride her again in the Yorkshire Oaks, took her on a seven-furlong spin up the Cambridge Road Polytrack gallop. The weather was filthy, but the *Racing Post*'s gallops reporter could see well enough, and under the headline 'OUIJA BOARD SETS GALLOPS ALIGHT IN YORK WARM-UP' wrote:

Ouija Board was settled behind her regular lead companion as connections viewed the action through driving rain, but when Fallon asked his mount to pick up the response was instantaneous as she skipped clear in most impressive fashion.

It was clearly all systems go for the Yorkshire Oaks, and for the first time we decided to take all three children with us to see Ouija Board race. They had been sharing the dream, and deserved the chance to see her run in the flesh. Our nanny Carole is from Yorkshire and very familiar with the York Railway Museum, to which the children were dispatched while we had what they would have considered 'a boring lunch' before the race.

But throughout the morning the weather worsened. It rained and rained and rained, and the York going, which had officially been 'good (good to soft in places)' for the opening day of the meeting, would certainly be soft. On arrival at the Knavesmire, Ed, Cazzy and I walked the course, and did not like what we saw – or rather felt. If we pushed a stick into the ground it went straight in: the going was bottomless, and would not suit Ouija Board at all. It was highly unlikely that we would risk running her in such conditions, but we decided to defer a decision until after the jockeys in the first race had come back and given their opinion – the Yorkshire Oaks was the fourth race on the programme, immediately after the nineteen-strong field for the Ebor Handicap would have galloped over the same ground – but we were in very pessimistic mood as we went off to have lunch with The Earl of Halifax, chairman of the York Race Committee. We realised that if we withdrew Ouija Board without the excuse of a change in the official going we would be fined, but the filly's interests had to come first, and she would hate these conditions. After the first race, a ten-furlong handicap run over much of the Yorkshire Oaks course, the jockeys reported the ground on the round course very soft, and we had no further need for discussion: out she came – and the official going was changed from 'good to soft' in the morning to 'soft', so we were spared the fine. I was not popular when I arrived back in the York Race Committee lunch room and said what I had done.

It was desperately sad, most immediately for our children and all the other Ouija Board connections but also for the massive crowd which make the York August Meeting one of the most vibrant occasions of the racing year. Losing the hot favourite from the day's big race so late on was very disappointing, but there was more to the on-course reaction than that. Ouija Board was the day's star turn, the sort of horse who puts a spring in the step of the most world-weary racegoer, and she was already evincing the sort of devotion and affection which over the next two seasons would grow, and would spread around the world. In her absence the Yorkshire Oaks went to Prince Khalid Abdullah's filly Quiff, who with Kieren Fallon on board won by eleven lengths from Pongee, and the following month finished runner-up to Rule Of Law in the St Leger, beaten by a head. The fact that Quiff won the Yorkshire Oaks by such a margin, and that the rest of the field finished very strung out – the distances between the eight runners were eleven, one and a half, nine, eight, four, twenty-one and five lengths! – really illustrated how bad the ground was that day.

Ouija Board went back to Newmarket, and we went back to discussing where next.

The Prix Vermeille at Longchamp on the day of the so-called 'Arc trials' in mid-September was one option, but we discarded that and decided to go straight to the Prix de l'Arc de Triomphe meeting on the first weekend of October. Ed favoured the Prix de l'Opera, a Group 1 event confined to fillies, while I was set on the Arc itself, one of the greatest races in the world and one in which Ouija Board would for the first time take on the cream of older horses, colts as well as fillies. This was the first time that Ed and I had disagreed over Ouija Board's programme: understandably he wanted to go for the best opportunity of landing a Group 1 race with her,

while I thought it would be more fun to be part of the main event. After all, Ouija Board was not trying to preserve a flawless record, and there would be no stigma in being beaten in such a race. I was a relatively new kid on the block who simply wanted the fun of being able to say, 'I've got a runner in the Arc', and I never wanted anyone to be able to say that we had been in any way timid in the way we had campaigned our filly. It is the prerogative of the owner to have the final say, and my final say was to go for the Arc. (The trainer can then blame the silly owner when it all goes wrong, and can insist that he wanted to run in the other race all along!) And for his part, Peter supported me in going for the Arc.

Such a decision meant that we could no longer have the services of Kieren Fallon, who had got on so well with Ouija Board and had ridden her so perfectly in her three races of the 2004 season, as he was committed to riding that year's Derby winner North Light for Ballymacoll Stud and Sir Michael Stoute. Frankie Dettori was claimed by Godolphin for Mamool and most of the top French jockeys were already spoken. For one of the world's big races you really need a proper big-race jockey, and Longchamp is a notoriously difficult course to ride, so we were fortunate to get Johnny Murtagh, who is not only one of the world's leading riders but had already won the Arc on Sinndar in 2000. His combination of big-race temperament and Arc experience seemed to suit us well, the only potential problem being that he had not ridden Ouija Board before, and by then we were aware that for a jockey she took some knowing: her tendency to drop herself out in the early stages

So near in the Arc: Ouija Board just fails to reach Bago and Cherry Mix.

sometimes made it difficult to work out exactly the right tactics: her great strength was her turn of foot, and the knack was to know exactly when to deploy it.

Again we chartered a plane, into which this time we put no fewer than ten members of Team Ouija Board: Cazzy and myself, Ed and Becky, Peter and his wife Frances, our sister Diana and her boyfriend (now husband) Nick Edwards, and Cazzy's sister Amanda and her husband Stephen Murray; my mother Rosie and stepfather Bill Spiegelberg had flown out the day before.

After a convivial lunch at Longchamp I bumped into the Aga Khan, who had two of the previous four runnings of the Arc with Sinndar and Dalakhani but who this time did not have a runner. He told me how much he was looking forward to seeing Ouija Board again, and how in an interview for French television he had talked up our filly as a wonderfully brave and exceptionally talented contender, and the horse he hoped would win.

A typically high-class field included the winners of all three major European Derbys – North Light (Derby), Grey Swallow (Irish Derby) and Blue Canari (Prix du Jockey-Club) – along with such luminaries as Bago (who had run third in the Juddmonte International at York after winning the Grand Prix de Paris at Longchamp),

Warrsan (who had won his second Coronation Cup at Epsom immediately before Ouija Board's Oaks), the four-year-old filly Pride (an unlucky third in the Prix Vermeille), Valixir (winner of the Prix Niel) and the Japanese challenger Tap Dance City (who had won the Japan Cup in 2003). Ouija Board started third favourite, with only North Light and Grey Swallow preferred in the betting at so-called industry prices.

After three glorious exhibitions of everything going right for Ouija Board, the Arc was the day when things went wrong. As usual she was held up, but instead of being 'dropped in' she ended up being more 'dropped out', with the result that coming into the straight she was much further back than was comfortable, and we watched in horror as she then encountered all sorts of traffic problems as Johnny Murtagh tried desperately to line her up for her run. A furlong and a half out he managed to get clear, but Bago and Cherry Mix had already settled down to battle out the lead, and though Ouija Board came flying down the stands side unbelievably fast, she could not quite get to them and had to settle for third, beaten 1½ lengths by Bago, trained by French-based but English-born Jonathan Pease. (Jonathan's mother Rosie and my mother Rosie, who knew each other years ago, met up again at Longchamp and for the next two years would ring each other whenever the respective horses were running, and my mother even received a Christmas card signed 'Granny Bago'!)

At the time we were not downhearted. She had run a wonderful race, and in being narrowly beaten in such company had enhanced her reputation considerably. Yet at the same time she had seemed unfortunate to lose, a view shared by the experts on the *Racing Post*:

If ever there was an unlucky loser it was Ouija Board. She was shuffled back in the big field and had to wait for a gap so that she was well adrift starting to make her move. She did very well to get into contention on the outside but then could find no extra close home as the effort of getting into the race took its toll ... She will be a four-year-old to look forward to.

That last sentence was indeed heartening, and while we felt temporarily a little deflated by what had happened, we now knew yet another aspect of Ouija Board: that as well as being the best of her age and sex, she could seriously compete with the colts at the highest level. I was even more proud of her than before. After all, she had beaten three Derby winners, and by the end of her career plenty of experts – Peter among them – still considered the 2004 Arc her finest performance of all.

Some people said we were unlucky, to which my response was that if third place in the Arc is unlucky, then give me unlucky any day. Truly unlucky is not being able to run at all, like the Cheveley Park Stud's mare Chorist, who was due to fly to Paris from Cambridge airport on the same plane as Ouija Board, but had become very agitated when being loaded, had banged his head and was forced to return home.

(A couple of weeks later, when the dust from the Arc excitement had settled, our then six-year-old son Edward, who loves racing and has always followed Ouija Board's career keenly, rushed into the room to find Cazzy. 'Mama, Mama, come and look at the Arc again!', he urged, and hurried her to the nursery where he had been watching a recording of the race. 'Look! Johnny Murtagh didn't give her a bad ride at all. With such a large field she just got stuck in a traffic jam!')

Once we had realised that in Ouija Board we had a horse who could race in the best company anywhere in the world, Ed was very keen that we should consider the Breeders' Cup, in 2004 being held for the first time at Lone Star Park, near Dallas, Texas. I was less convinced than Ed that this was a sensible step, as I was thinking about the entry fee of $90,000; the huge cost of flying her across and back (while for some big overseas races all the horse's and connections' expenses are covered by the host country, you pay your own way for the Breeders' Cup); how much a ten-hour flight would take out of her; how she would respond to a completely alien racecourse; and, not least, how she would react to being taken out of the cool of an English autumn and landed in the heat of Texas. I am not a betting man, but taking Ouija Board on such a trip would in effect be staking tens of thousands of pounds on a venture whose outcome was far from certain.

As before the Oaks and before the Arc, there was a great deal of debate among members of the team about whether to go or not, and at one point my brother Peter underlined his determination that she should go to Texas by offering to pay her entry fee himself. (Peter rightly points out that, during the debates between him, Ed, Cazzy and myself about which race we should

go for, each of us called right at some point and wrong at others.) Ed was extremely keen to attempt the Breeders' Cup, a point he impressed strongly upon Peter during a long chat at the yearling sales at Tattersalls in Newmarket, and Peter called Cazzy to recommend that all available pressure should be brought to bear on her husband.

Her golden opportunity came about in an unexpected manner. I pulled some ligaments while playing tennis at Knowsley, which left me on crutches for several days, and when one evening I was in the bath, Cazzy – who had been told by Ed that she had to get me to agree to run Ouija Board in Texas – came in and moved my crutches out of reach, threatening not to give them back unless there and then I committed Ouija Board to Lone Star Park.

That settled it. I got the crutches back, and we were Texas-bound.

On one point there could be no disagreement whatsoever – that for a European-trained horse to win a Breeders' Cup race was a huge achievement. This one amazing racing day, held each autumn at a different course in North America, was inaugurated in 1984 and was soon being billed as 'The World Thoroughbred Racing Championships'. Although Clive Brittain-trained Pebbles won the Breeders' Cup Turf in 1985 to notch an early score for British horses, Dancing Brave was sensationally beaten in the same race in California the following year, and it took some while for the event to be a natural entry on the later-season agenda for English horses. Some years attracted a bigger British entry than others – our horses seemed to be better suited to New

York courses than the heat of California or Florida – and 2004 saw an entry of only two British-based horses, the smallest in Breeders' Cup history. Both were trained in Newmarket, with the Jeremy Noseda-trained two-year-old Wilko, who was going for the Breeders' Cup Juvenile, and Ouija Board, aiming at the Breeders' Cup Filly and Mare Turf.

Long-haul international travel for racehorses and for their connections is a complicated business, and for the first of Ouija Board's trips to another continent we were singularly blessed for both the equine and the human arrangements. The filly's own travel plans – which involved such matters as quarantine as well as the huge logistical jigsaw of flying across the Atlantic and arriving in fit state to do herself justice – were looked after by Peden, where Lucy Greayer was to become a vital cog in the Ouija Board machine. For the first time our filly was accompanied on her travels by Brian Taylor, who would act as her flying groom – a highly specialised role involving everything to do with transporting the horse to the airport, overseeing the loading into the place, monitoring wellbeing through the flight and seeing the horse safely arrived at the destination – for all her international travels. Flying a racehorse to another country, while much more straightforward than it was thirty years ago, remains a major logistical exercise which in the case of Ouija Board included such considerations as flying out her own feed and hay in advance to ensure that they had cleared customs in time. Horses have delicate stomachs: a change of diet could prove

disastrous, and to avoid the risk involved in a change of water, racecourses provided bottled water for visiting horses.

Brian Taylor – son of the late jockey of the same name – was to grow very close to Ouija Board over the years, and his presence on every step of her journeys played a large part in her international achievements.

In Texas, Ouija Board had the familiar figures of Chris Hinson (who at the time rode her in all her exercise at home and abroad) and travelling head lad Robin Trevor-Jones with her constantly, and both were core members of the team. Robin accompanied her on every one of her overseas trips, both within Europe and further afield.

A pick of grass in the Texan sun at evening stables, with Cazzy and Tracy Potter in attendance.

For our part, we were looked after in the USA by Alastair Donald and Adrian Beaumont from the Newmarket-based International Racing Bureau, which has long been an invaluable aid to connections of British-based horses in pursuit of international prizes (and they were being assisted for this Breeders' Cup by Christina McKenzie – now Christina Dunlop, wife of Ed's brother Harry). The internationalisation of racing has accelerated considerably over the last two decades, and the way in which the IRB has lubricated the process has been an important contributory factor both to the growing bullishness of British and other European connections going for big races in far-flung parts of the globe, and to the undoubted success – not to mention prize money – which that adventurous spirit has brought.

The Filly and Mare Turf, in the eight-race Breeders' Cup programme one of three events run on turf rather than dirt, had been introduced to the card in 1999, and had already been won by two notable European challengers: Banks Hill, trained in France by Andre Fabre, at Belmont Park, New York, in 2001, and Sir Michael Stoute-trained Islington at Santa Anita, California, in 2003.

From the European point of view, the great imponderable of the 2004 Breeders' Cup was its location. While English owners and trainers had become used to regular venues such as Churchill Downs or Belmont Park, for the first time the event was being staged at the unfamiliar Lone Star Park, near Dallas in Texas.

The entry system for the Breeders' Cup means that, having paid the entry fee, you can leave open the choice of race until three days before, and while we were committed to going across, there remained a possibility that Ouija Board would take on the colts in the Breeders' Cup Turf over 1½ miles rather than go for the furlong shorter race restricted to fillies and mares. But we decided to stick with our initial inclination: the Filly and Mare Turf.

A Victory Celebration

Running Ouija Board on a different continent was a step into the unknown on more than one front. The form of the leading American fillies and mares likely to be opposing her was pretty well wholly unknown to me, and here the assistance of Ed's racing secretary Peter Shoemark was invaluable. Peter's duties at Gainsborough

Chris Hinson and 'Mother' relax at morning exercise.

My first experience of trackwork in the USA: Kieren and Ouija Board stretch their legs in the early morning.

Stables cover the whole gamut of administrative functions essential in a big, modern training yard – such as registering and monitoring entries – and he is astoundingly well versed in the form of the leading horses around the globe. In the run-up to Lone Star Park I spent many hours on the phone to him, discussing who our likely rivals would be and the niceties of the form lines. Peter has been another vital member of the Ouija Board team, as has another stalwart of Gainsborough Stables, Ed's secretary Angela Lowe, who for our filly's overseas ventures has been tireless in making all the essential arrangements. A huge amount of credit is also due to Liz Cowdy, Andrea Poole and Sarah Maitland-Titterton, our PA's who cheerfully, and often at very short notice, helped with the complicated travel plans of the ever-increasing Team Ouija.

Despite all this back-up, our foray to Texas made me feel like a nervous schoolboy starting out at a new school, and we were hugely fortunate in the USA to be assisted at every turn by the wonderful Pamela BlatzMurff, one of the senior vice-presidents of Breeders' Cup Inc., who looked after our every need for the duration of our stay – and who by the end of Ouija Board's globe-trotting career had become completely established as another key member of the team.

For its first Breeders' Cup, Lone Star Park

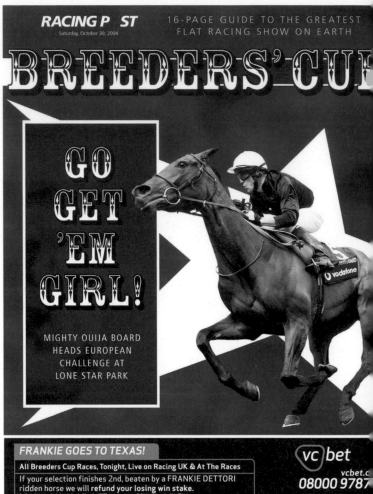

understandably wanted to push the boat out, and, fittingly for the state which prides itself on being bigger and better than every other in the USA, nothing was done by halves. I have an

Breeders' Cup Filly and Mare Turf, 2004: Home encouragement from the Racing Post front page is rewarded as Ouija Board comes wide round the final turn with Film Maker (centre) and Moscow Burning ... then quickens clear to win from Film Maker and Wonder Again.

A unusual view of the Filly and Mare Turf finish, taken from the infield, shows the extensive temporary stands necessary at both ends of the permanent grandstand to accommodate the huge Lone Star Park crowd.

abiding memory of the press party on the Thursday night, where every local was dressed in style from the huge Stetson downwards – cowboy shirt, belt with a gigantic ornamental buckle, jeans and cowboy boots. There must have been at least a thousand people there, beer flowed all night, and the music was provided by the great country singer Willie Nelson. Among the other attractions was a mechanical Bucking Bronco which some of us tried to ride – and the 2004 Dunlop Christmas card featured the six of us (Derbys, Stanleys and Dunlops) astride this fearsome machine.

If the Texas hospitality was wonderful, the Texas weather seemed to be turning against us. Heavy rainstorms had bombarded the track – exactly what Ouija Board did not want – and we spent an anxious couple of days before it started to dry out. Then the heat was compounded by humidity, along with which came insects who took a fancy to Ouija Board and constantly bit her. We could treat the bites with insect repellent, but had to very careful that any medication did not risk transgressing the rules about drugs which applied in Texas, and therefore to the Texas-based Breeders' Cup.

We hired a stretch limo, a new experience for most of us, to take us from our hotel to the course. We were very nervous so the buffet lunch was preceded by a couple of Bloody Marys,

in what was to become a pre-race ritual which, with due superstition, we felt duty bound to continue before future races (even though I do not like Bloody Marys!). Then, after a hefty slice

of excellent chocolate gateau, we settled into our six-seater 'loge' (like a cattle pen) in the stands to watch the early races. The first event on turf was the Breeders' Cup Mile, and it terrified all of us to see how tight the turns were: I have to confess that the circuit put me in mind of a dog track. It seemed a miracle that no horse fell or seriously slipped, and contemplating how Ouija Board

who had finished runner-up to Casual Look in the previous year's Oaks after winning the Irish One Thousand Guineas, and Aubonne from France were the only other European challengers, and I knew little about the nine home-based runners.

The race itself was fairly straightforward. Ouija Board was always in touch, moved into fourth place at about halfway, was third into the straight, took the lead with more than a furlong to go, and only had to be pushed out by Kieren to win easily by a length and a half from Film Maker. The *Racing Post* declared:

Two British raiders for the Breeders' Cup, two British winners – and two triumphant jockeys, Kieren Fallon and Frankie Dettori, at the post-race celebration.

might come round those bends really put the wind up us, with Cazzy and Becky simultaneously saying, 'She's not a motorbike!'

She was always travelling with ease before being brought wide off the home turn and quickening impressively in the straight for a cosy success on ground slower than ideal. This stamped her among the best fillies in the world, and the best at her distance, so the decision to swerve the Turf and take up this challenge was a smart move by connections. Set to stay in training, she could hit even greater heights as a four-year-old ...

Amen to that!

The Filly and Mare Turf was the fifth Breeders' Cup race, two races after the Mile, and when we went down to see Ouija Board in the crowded paddock she looked such a picture that I started to feel a little more optimistic. Kieren was back on board and we were very hopeful, a feeling clearly shared by many of the Lone Star Park betting public, who sent her off at odds on – which certainly surprised me.

Aidan O'Brien's four-year-old filly Yesterday,

I heard later during the race an American television channel had a camera trained on a gentleman who they thought was Lord Derby, and after making observations about how, for the winning owner, he did not look very pleased, the presenter had to conclude: 'Lord Derby does not look very happy at his victory ... He is totally unmoved ... In fact, I'm not sure we're on Lord Derby.' They can't have been, for the real Lord Derby was extremely pleased, and, as so often in Ouija Board's career, made no attempt to disguise his rapture.

The Cartier Awards Dinner: receiving Ouija Board's Horse of the Year trophy from Arnaud Bamberger, who runs Cartier in the UK.

By the end of the afternoon Wilko, owned by Paul Roy (who in January 2007 became the first chairman of the new Horseracing Regulatory Authority), had won the Juvenile under Frankie to complete a wonderful double for the English challenge: two runners, two winners. That evening the two camps – including both winning jockeys – joined forces in the bar of our hotel to stage an impromptu celebration party, but we were up in time the following morning to visit Ouija Board in her barn – as usual she showed no ill effects from her race – and go to the post-Breeders' Cup press breakfast.

Then we made a dash for the airport, pausing only to stop the car and run into a clothing store to get the whole team fitted out with the appropriate Texan gear – souvenirs of a memorable visit. And the poor British Airways staff had to cope with our taking on as hand luggage the huge flower garland put on Ouija Board after her victory!

Back in England, we were again awash with messages of congratulation. Winning a Breeders' Cup race was a very special achievement indeed for Ouija Board, and our delight was shared by so many others. Again a letter from Sir Mark Prescott is worth quoting:

My Lord,

Just a brief and inadequate note to say how much I, and the whole of Newmarket, enjoyed your famous victory in the Breeders' Cup last night. You would be so gratified to know how the whole town has savoured the occasion.

I went to a Breeders' Cup supper last night and the whole room was jumping and screaming to cheer your champion filly on – almost as much as the trainer did, judging from the television coverage!

Her whole career has been faultlessly handled by owner, breeder, stud manager, trainer and jockey(s) – an admirable lesson to us all in how to nurture the best talents to the full.

Young Ed has set us all some target to aim at in the seasons to come.

Then the awards season was upon us.

The Cartier Awards Dinner is organised by Arnaud Bamberger and Harry Herbert, the driving force behind Highclere Thoroughbreds and the Royal Ascot Racing Club, who always gives a hilarious speech, and the award for Three-Year-Old Filly of the Year lay between Ouija Board, who had won three Group 1 races, and the marvellous Attraction, who had won four: One Thousand Guineas, Irish One Thousand Guineas, Coronation Stakes and (newly elevated to Group 1) Sun Chariot Stakes, and the moment of the announcement was neatly caught by Carl Evans in the *Directory of the Turf 2005*:

'And the winner of the most unwanted-job-in-racing award goes to' ... the judges who had to decide between Ouija Board and Attraction for Cartier's three-year-old filly title.

The merits of two much-loved, home-bred, dual Classic winners, each with a fairytale aspect to their careers, must have been extremely difficult to separate, but once the experts had plumped for Lord Derby's Ouija Board their next task was easy, and they duly made her Horse of the Year as well.

When pondering what might have swung the judges for Three-Year-Old Filly of the year our way, I assumed that the clincher for Ouija Board was her terrific effort against the colts in the Arc. Attraction ran against the opposite sex only once in 2004, when last on unsuitable going in the Prix Jacques le Marois at Deauville.

Then came the Racehorse Owners' Association Awards, at which Guy Roxburghe and I agreed to take a table together at the awards dinner. Again Ouija Board was named Outstanding Three-Year-Old Filly and Horse of the Year, and to my delight I was named Owner of the Year – a great honour to be voted for by my fellow ROA members. It was also a major honour for me to be named Owner of the Year at the Derby Awards staged by the Horserace Writers' and Photographers' Association in December: I do hope that Geoff Lester, who speculated about the odds against that happening back in June, was accommodated at a hefty price! And Ed

picked up the International Trainer of the Year award at the HWPA lunch.

On a less formal level, Rodney Masters in the *Racing Post* named Ouija Board his 'Darling of 2004', declaring that 'the darling of 2004 sent the wow factor spinning off the scale', and another *Post* journalist Lee Mottershead struck exactly the right note in his essay on Ouija Board in the book *Flat Horses of 2004*:

There is something rather wonderful about Ouija Board. It is because of her and because of the people around her. It is because of what she has done and because of the way she has done it. It is because of all the glorious little subplots that, combined, made her rise to stardom arguably the defining story of the 2004 British Flat season. It is because she made the year so much more enjoyable than it would have been without her – and because we have it all to look forward to again in 2005.

Such an amazing tale. Such an unlikely tale. The only racehorse to carry the colours of a distinguished English aristo, one of whose forebears gave his name to the sport's most famous race, she was victorious in the Classic first won by the same forebear 225 years earlier. A filly nobody outside her stable truly considered likely to be one of the season's leading lights at the start of the campaign, she went on to complete a famous Classic double before proving herself the best filly in Europe and then, on a spectacular day in Texas, the best turf filly in the world.

And in doing all this she triggered within her team scenes of such sincere, spontaneous and

The heroine's return to Gainsborough Stables.

uncontrollable joy that even the most hardened observer was softened. It is not just Lord Derby, Ed Dunlop and Kieren Fallon who owe a debt of gratitude to Ouija Board. We all do.

Lee's piece ended:

Based on simple handicapping assessment, Ouija Board is no superstar. But while she falls behind even some of her fellow three-year-olds in terms of official ratings, she has earned her place high on the list of Britain's finest ever fillies. Blessed with a tremendous turn of foot and searing acceleration, she is a dual Oaks winner who went on to fly the flag in the Breeders' Cup. As such, she deserves to be talked of in the same breath as the likes of Pebbles and Oh So Sharp, if only because of the impact she has made on, and pleasure she has given to, British racing fans.

A filly representing special people, she has become the people's filly, and the people's filly will be back again at four. The days of doffing caps to the aristocracy may be gone, but doff your proverbial cap to Ouija Board. She deserves that respect. She has done her country proud.

In this shower of adulation and awards ended Ouija Board's amazing three-year-old year, and, as it turned out, only the first leg of our wonderful journey with her. She had brought us three Group 1 victories and a heroic third in the Arc, and although we salivated at the thought of more to come, she was already, for us at least, a mare in a million.

CHAPTER THREE

'A MINOR MIRACLE'
THE 2005 SEASON

Although there had been some talk concerning whether Ouija Board might again spend the winter at Stanley House Stud, Ed was keen to keep her under his watchful eye at Gainsborough Stables, and we were happy to concur. Her presence at the stud might have been too much of a distraction for my staff, and Ed said that not long ago a good horse of his had gone wrong after going home for the winter.

There had been a number of big-money offers for Ouija Board immediately after she won the Pretty Polly Stakes, but we were never tempted. 'Money can't buy dreams,' Cazzy had acutely observed. It was obvious to all that we enjoyed every second of the experience of owning such a horse. Money simply had nothing to do with it, whereas spending the early months of 2005 working out her possible programme and monitoring he progress towards race fitness was an unquantifiable delight.

The awards continued to flow in. On 6 January it was announced that Ouija Board had been nominated for an Eclipse Award in the USA in two divisions: Three-Year-Old Filly and (along with Intercontinental and Tickertape) Filly and Mare Turf Specialist. By winning a Breeders' Cup race she garnered another American award, collected on our behalf by Bill Farish, an old friend of Peter's who ran the Lanes End stud farm in Kentucky: his father Will Farish, former US ambassador in London, had owned 2003 Oaks winner Casual Outlook.

Stanley House Stud was named Breeder of the Year 2004 in the Thoroughbred Breeders' Association Awards, and we were delighted that our table at the awards dinner included, along with Peter and Frances and my mother and stepfather, Pat Cronin and his wife, stud secretary Nancy Pollitt and her partner, and our vet Professor Sidney Ricketts and his wife. Like Mike Shepherd a partner in the Rossdales practice, Sidney had been vet to Stanley House Stud for twenty years, and his premature retirement on medical grounds was the end of a wonderful chapter of our breeding operation.

More excitement followed with the announcement of the Eclipse Awards results later

Peter Stanley accepts Ouija Board's first Eclipse Award.

in the month: Ouija Board had won the Filly and Mare Turf Specialist, netting 235 of the 274 votes cast by members of the National Turf Writers' Association. American racing takes the Eclipse Awards extremely seriously, and for our filly to win one after only one race in the USA was both thrilling and gratifying. She was now truly an international superstar. The awards ceremony took place in Beverly Hills, and since we were on holiday in Mauritius with the Dunlops, Peter and Frances were able to accept it on my behalf on their way to the Karaka Sales in New Zealand.

January also brought publication of the Thoroughbred World Rankings, a table of ratings based on pounds to be carried in some notional handicap designed to rank the world's top horses, and inaugurated to replace the previous International Classifications. Plotting the exact measure of Ouija Board's ability in some arid number has never held much appeal for me, though I appreciate that for various purposes within the bloodstock business a high figure is worth flaunting; however she has been officially or unofficially rated at any stage of career, that rating can convey nothing of the magic of her presence or the manner in which she raced. So it was with strictly academic interest that I read that these World Rankings had placed her on a mark of 120, eight pounds below top-rated Smarty Jones, the colt who had won the Kentucky Derby and Preakness Stakes, and seven pounds below her Arc conqueror Bago. Ouija Board was the leading three-year-old filly, but by these ratings she was joint twenty-eighth in the overall rank of world racehorses – a good deal below where she stood in the estimation of the Derby household!

Still the awards kept coming, with the British Horseracing Board recognising Ouija Board as both Three-Year-Old Filly and Horse of the Year. The latter award brought with it, unusually, a presentation to the horse itself in the form of a very fine horse-rug and surcingle, which is occasionally worn by Knowsley's resident rocking horse when it is moved into the dining room for the odd dinner party.

This flood of awards prompted me to write to the *Guinness Book of Records*, suggesting they include Ouija Board in their next edition as the recipient of the most awards in one year of any sporting figure. I received a stock reply spelling out the criteria and procedure for registering a new award in such tedious detail that I dropped the idea.

For all the joy that awards brought us, Ouija Board was a racehorse, and we had to think hard about her first race of 2005 – a prospect even more exciting after Kieren Fallon had come to ride work on her in the spring and pronounced that she had definitely trained on, as there is always the worry with a four-year-old filly that she will not reproduce the form she had shown at three.

At one point we hoped to run her in the Coronation Cup at Epsom on the same day as the Oaks, but then a 'splint' – a bony enlargement of one of the splint bones below the knee – was detected on her near foreleg. She needed rest, and would not be fit in time for Epsom; and in any case, with a long season ahead of us – the principal target was another Breeders' Cup appearance – there was no hurry.

Soon recovered from the splint, her recuperation greatly aided by sessions every evening in the ice spa, Ouija Board now had her sights set on the Prince of Wales's Stakes at Royal Ascot, which in 2005 was moved to York while the awe-inspiring new grandstand at the Berkshire course was being built. Had I been

Synchronised galloping: Julie Lingham on False Promise heads Chris Hinson on 'Mother' on the Cambridge Road Polytrack gallop at Newmarket, March 2005. I don't know how Ed teaches his charges to keep exact step!

Ouija Board on the Newmarket training grounds: left, with Chris Hinson on a misty morning (William Knight, Ed's assistant, in the background); above, a debriefing by Jamie Spencer to Chris and Ed during her preparation for Royal Ascot at York.

overly concerned with omens I might have baulked at sending her to York again after the deep disappointment of taking her there for the Yorkshire Oaks and then not running. As it was we had more specific worries. She had suffered a 'quarter crack' – a small crack at the top of her hoof – on her near fore foot, which was not in itself serious but meant that the usual nails could not be used to secure her shoe to that hoof: at York she would have to run in a

specially fitted plastic shoe glued to her foot.

Another and potentially deeper worry was that the York going was in so bad a condition that at one point it seemed likely the jockeys would refuse to ride on it. Rain falling on ground which had already been watered caused a loosening of the turf, and on the Tuesday, the first day of the meeting – the Prince of Wales's Stakes was on the Wednesday – several horses had slipped up on the home turn. The principal remedial work had been the application of a large amount of sand, and while the first day's programme was completed without a major incident, I was still profoundly worried about racing Ouija Board on ground which the jockeys reported as being firm underneath but loose on top.

My fears were compounded by persistent rain on the Wednesday morning. We had been invited to have lunch with The Queen and her party at nearby Bishopsthorpe Palace, the official residence of The Archbishop of York, and beforehand I had left a phone message at the racecourse for York's chief executive William Derby (no relation) to let me have the latest news on the state of the ground. He rang back just as I was arriving at the palace, so I had to dive straight into the loo to take the call. William assured me that the ground would be fine, but as I emerged from the bathroom I was greeted by one of Her Majesty's ladies-in-waiting, clearly worried that I had suffered a stomach upset and was anxious to know whether I was all right. I assured her that all was well, and that it was only the going which was causing me perturbations!

Following lunch we were granted the great honour of travelling down the course by carriage in the Royal Procession – though on account of the rain the carriages had to be covered over. I sat next to Chica, wife of Harry Herbert – who has made such an impact with his racing syndicates such as Highclere Thoroughbreds, and whose brainchild the Royal Ascot Racing Club had earlier that month scored a stunning victory with Motivator in the Derby – and we were clearly able to see all the sand that had been applied to the course.

So it was an anxious party of Ouija Board connections who waited in the parade ring for our heroine to come in – led up for the first time by her new groom Pat Evens, who had got to know the filly when looking after her on the weekends and days when Tracy Potter was off. Tracy had left Ed's yard before Ouija Board's four-year-old season had got under way, and daily care of the then stable star was entrusted to Pat, a lady with a huge amount of experience: she was some time with trainer Geoffrey Barling before spending seventeen years in the Newmarket yard of the late John Winter, after which she had moved for a period to South Africa. Pat's devotion to Ouija Board was total, and her calm presence with our filly from well before the crack of dawn each morning was infectious, Ouija Board responding in like manner. There was a real bond between the two of them.

The Prince of Wales's Stakes, in which Ouija Board was reunited with Jamie Spencer for the first time since her final race as a two-year-old, attracted a stellar field headed by the Aga Khan's Azamour, who had won the St James's Palace Stakes at the Royal meeting the previous year; Aidan O'Brien trained Ace; Norse Dancer, who was so often placed but never won in Group 1 company; Warrsan, the dual Coronation Cup winner still in training as a seven-year-old; and Elvestroem, a globe-trotting Australian-trained horse who had won a big race on Dubai World Cup day in the spring and most recently had finished runner-up to Valixir in the Prix d'Ispahan at Longchamp. Azamour started 11-8 favourite, with Ouija Board, ridden by Jamie Spencer, second favourite at 7-2, having opened in the betting at 5-2.

The race did not go happily for us. Early in the race the stick-on shoe was pulled off by the

Gloom — with more to come: Jamie Spencer takes Ouija Board to post before the Prince of Wales's Stakes at York, 15 June 2005.

Horse and groom in perfect harmony:
Pat Evens with her beloved charge.

Flowers from her owner during recuperation.

glutinous going, and after that Ouija Board was never travelling well enough to give us any hope, eventually trailing in seventh of the eight runners behind Azamour. Ed was asked by the stewards' secretary to account for her poor showing, and his explanation that she had lost a shoe and was unsuited by the ground (which that day was officially described as 'Good to firm') was accepted.

Had all of us known all of the facts and everybody else's opinion, would we have run her? We can never know, but hindsight gives a different perspective, and for his part, Ed is entirely frank: 'I think the whole occasion got to us and affected our judgement. On reflection, I regretted running her.'

Then came the big blow. Even allowing for the loss of the shoe and her dislike of the ground,

Ouija Board had run, by her standards, a dismal race. Was there some further explanation? Back in Newmarket, Ed's wonderful vet Mike Shepherd did a full veterinary examination, which included a nuclear bone scan on her near foreleg, and it was revealed that she had sustained a stress fracture to her near fore cannon bone, the bone between the knee and the fetlock. (This was a totally separate injury from the splint bone.) She would be out of action for weeks, maybe months – and maybe she would be out of action for good. (York is a fantastic racecourse, and for a great many so lucky; sadly it just seems to be an unlucky racecourse for me.)

This was deeply depressing. For Ed's staff, who were all borne along by Ouija Board's success and who all, in one way or another, contributed to it, it was a major blow to morale. They were devoted to Ouija Board, and knew that there might never again be a horse as good in the yard – and now they had to face the harsh truth that she might never run again. Whether they are directly concerned with the individual horse or not, stable staff are given a huge fillip by having a star in their care, and reverses such as this are profoundly felt.

For myself and Cazzy, this sequence of setbacks – splint, then quarter crack, then stress fracture – served as a kick back into the realities of racehorse ownership after the heady days of Ouija Board's three-year-old career. I heard a member of one the big racing operations suggest that she had not trained on from three to four, but for the most part the news of her injury was greeted with great sympathy for us and a wish that she would be seen again later in the year.

Ouija Board went back to Gainsborough Stables and all plans for future races were on hold, the only priority being to nurse her back to health.

Time passed and the season wore on. Races such as the King George VI and Queen Elizabeth Diamond Stakes – run that year at Newbury – and the Nassau Stakes at Goodwood, which might have been on the agenda, took place without her. Early in August came light at the end of the tunnel. A full scan of the affected area in Ouija

Ouija Board the star attraction at Ed's open day.

Board's leg was taken by Mike Shepherd, who pronounced himself satisfied that the injury had healed, and she started back in ridden exercise. On 10 August she was ridden in a good piece of work by Jamie Spencer – then well on his way to becoming champion jockey for the first time – and the *Racing Post* front-page reported, 'Ouija Board delight after "critical" gallop.' Nine days later Jamie rode her again in a gallop on the Polytrack circuit at Lingfield Park racecourse, which we came through with our anxious hopes for a return to proper action strengthened: we

*In the Newmarket pre-parade ring before the
Princess Royal Stakes, 24 September 2005.*

were becoming increasingly optimistic, but knew that it was still far from certain that the dark days were over.

Her level of activity was steadily increased, and on 25 August the gallops report in the *Racing Post* read: 'Ouija Board appeared to be nearing her optimum on the Cambridge Road Polytrack yesterday when, reunited with her groom Chris Hinson following her spin at Lingfield last Thursday, she enjoyed herself upsides Blythe Knight.'

Ouija Board's gradual return to race fitness was also being picked up by *Racing Post* columnist Peter Thomas, who early in September wrote:

It's against my nature to feel sorry for a peer of the realm who owns a horse who won two Classics and Breeders' Cup last year, but I'm beginning to wonder if Lord Derby ran over a black cat during the winter and had it made into a hat for his wife.

There must be some good reason for the run of bad luck he's had this season with Ouija Board, who was forced to miss her intended engagement at Newmarket on Saturday by the latest in a line of setbacks that's now nearly as long as his driveway.

Shin splints, bruised heel, foot in a hole, lost shoe, sore throat – it's surely only a matter of time before she walks under the window cleaner's ladder and gets hit by a flying bucket. This will probably happen two days before the Prix Vermeille, which has been named as the new, new starting point for her season proper.

This bleak period must come as something of

a culture shock to connections after a glittering end to 2004, during which the popping of champagne corks and flash bulbs accompanied their every move at each awards ceremony worthy of the name.

Trainer Ed Dunlop has yet to assault anybody for being the 100th person to ask him 'How's the filly?' on any given day, but his patience must be wearing thin.

I, for one, am itching for him to be able to give the answer: 'She's just great. No problems. The Vermeille and the Arc were nice races to win, but a second Breeders' Cup is what we really want and she's bang on course for Belmont.'

As a gesture on my part, I have just slaughtered the family's pet rabbit and all four of its feet will be arriving at Gainsborough Stables by first-class post tomorrow morning.

There was no way she was going to attempt a second Breeders' Cup without a prep race, and Ed and I started considering our options, discussing them at length. One possibility had been the September Stakes at Newmarket's July Course (relocated from Kempton Park while the Flat track at that course was being transmuted into an all-weather circuit) on the first weekend of September, but this seemed a little early, and was several weeks before the Breeders' Cup. Then Ouija Board coughed after a gallop and an endoscope examination showed a minor lung infection, so she was put back on the easy list for another fortnight. The Prix de l'Arc de Triomphe would be far too arduous a contest for her comeback race, and we were bent on keeping her fresh for America.

Eventually we decided that the Princess Royal Stakes, a race over 1½ miles usually run at Ascot but moved in 2005 to Newmarket and run on 24 September on the same afternoon as the Queen Elizabeth II Stakes, would be ideal. A Group 3 race, it was unlikely to provide excessively tough opposition, and as the principal aim was to confirm that she was restored to full health and had recaptured her form, that was a major consideration. After the unfortunate experience at York this was, in effect, her first race of the season, and it was a nerve-wracking

Back in the winning groove: Ouija Board and Frankie Dettori ease home in the Princess Royal Stakes at Newmarket.

Frankie, who tends to confine his acrobatics to Group 1 races, shows what he thinks of winning the Group 3 Princess Royal.

rides for my uncle John but never won a race for him, so had ridden in the colours – and literally the same set of silks, as after the Oaks victory we kept an old set of Derby colours for the exclusive use on Ouija Board for the rest of her racing career: exactly how old these silks are I cannot say, but they certainly seem to hark back to a time when jockeys had far less length of arm, as they look distinctly short in the sleeve on today's jockeys!

In a field of thirteen for the Princess Royal John Doyle Stakes, Ouija Board started 11-8 favourite, evidence that the betting public at least still had some faith in her. Some close to her at home had no doubt that she was back to her best. Chris Hinson, who was riding her in all her work, knew that while she was not at the very peak of fitness he could still feel the old magic: he considered her 'an absolute certainty' for the Princess Royal Stakes and backed her accordingly, as did Pat Cronin at the Stanley House Stud. Ed himself was characteristically more cautious, letting it be known that in his opinion, 'Either she'll hack up or she'll be last.'

It turned out to be the former, as the *Raceform* observer noted:

Ouija Board bounced back following the injury and various other problems that have kept her off the course for much of the season. She travelled easily, as a Group 1 filly at this level should, and looked like winning by a wide margin when striking the front. However, she had to be kept up to her work, and although she scored comfortably enough in the end, the form is a long way off her best.

time for all concerned. Ed recalls: 'She had shown us the right signs, but there was everything to lose and not much to gain. I was acutely aware that this might have been the last time she ever ran.'

With Kieren Fallon unavailable, we engaged Frankie Dettori for his first ride on Ouija Board. This was the first time Frankie had ridden for me, though he told me that he had had a number of

Indeed it was, but she won easily enough by 2½ lengths from Briolette, and the main thing was that she was back, and back in one piece.

Frankie – who was so thrilled to have won on her that he gave one of his famous flying dismounts in the winner's enclosure, a performance he usually restricts to Group 1 victories – reported that he had got to the front too soon, and it is certainly the case that each new jockey has seemed to take a while to tune in to Ouija Board, to appreciate that she has one sweeping run, and you should hold it until you need it. But this was no time to quibble, and after the race there was a wonderful mood in our party, a feeling of a job well done, a huge sense of relief that she was back on track, with her ability and her enthusiasm intact. No one was happier than our son Edward, then seven years old, who after the great disappointment of not seeing Ouija Board run at York the previous August was at Newmarket to see her race in the flesh for the first time.

The Newmarket victory was also a major boost for the Gainsborough Stables staff and for

In the winner's enclosure after the Princess Royal. The children are (left to right) our elder son Edward Stanley, nephew Hugh Stanley, nieces Isabella and Laura Murray, nephew Algy Stanley and niece Isobel Stanley.

the vets Rossdales, whose consummate care and attention had ensured her return to health and fitness.

It was all systems go for the autumn campaign overseas, but meanwhile Ouija Board had a more parochial duty to perform: lending her name, along with that of Wilko, her fellow British-trained Breeders' Cup winner in 2004, to the Cumberland Lodge Stakes, run on the second day of that Ascot meeting at Newmarket. Wilko's owner Paul Roy and I are both vice-presidents of the Veterinary School at the University of Liverpool, and it was Paul's idea to name the race after our respective stars to promote the School.

Ouija Board flew out to New York six days before the big day, and settled well into the quarantine barn at Belmont Park. Then the rains came, and for the second year running the *Racing Post* build-up during Breeders' Cup week was

Breeders' Cup, 2005: Jerry Bailey gets acquainted with Ouija Board.

dominated by what the going would be, and how the rain would affect our chances. The headlines tell the story:

Tuesday: 'EUROPEANS CONCERNED OVER THREAT OF MORE HEAVY RAIN'
Thursday: 'OUIJA BOARD GIVEN DIFFICULT OUTSIDE DRAW'
Friday: 'DUNLOP HAS HIGH HOPES OUIJA BOARD CAN DEFY SOFT GOING'
Saturday: 'CAUTIOUS OPTIMISM IN OUIJA BOARD CAMP'

Both the climate and the racetrack at Belmont were more suitable to British horses than Lone Star Park, and while there had been only two British-trained raiders in 2004 – and both had won – this time a far larger European contingent went across, including the likes of Bago, Shirocco and Ace, all of whom were running in the Breeders' Cup Turf, and Valixir and Ad Valorem in the Mile. With Kieren Fallon claimed to ride Mona Lisa for Coolmore in the Filly and Mare Turf and Frankie on Sundrop for Godolphin, we booked the top American jockey Jerry Bailey to ride Ouija Board, and a couple of days before the race he rode her round the track and pronounced himself pleased with the feel he had given her. Jerry's record in Breeders' Cup races was superb – before 2005 he had ridden fourteen winners, more than any other jockey in the history of the event – and he had got off Intercontinental, his original ride in the race, in order to ride our filly. Intercontinental had never raced over a distance as far as the ten furlongs she would be facing at Belmont Park, and Jerry was convinced that she would not stay. This was to prove an unfortunate misjudgement.

As always, Ouija Board looked magnificent on the day of the race, and went off 23-10 favourite in a field of fourteen which included Film Maker, runner-up to her in the 2004 race. In addition to Ouija Board, Mona Lisa and Sundrop, the European challenge included Favourable Terms from Sir Michael Stoute's yard, John Gosden-trained Karen's Caper, and Luas Line, trained in Ireland by David Wachman. On balance, it seemed a stronger line-up than in 2004.

The story of the race can be told simply. Intercontinental went into the lead as soon as the gates opened and remained there, with the other jockeys content to let her go until they thought they had better close the gap, by which time it was too late. Ouija Board came from off the pace early in the home stretch to go third with a quarter of a mile to race and then, with more than a furlong still to cover, into second , but although she ran on with her customary resolution, she could not get to Intercontinental and was beaten 1¼ lengths, with Film Maker third, again one place behind our filly. So much for Jerry Bailey's

Breeders' Cup Filly and Mare Turf, 2005: Ouija Board and Jerry Bailey make their move.

conviction that Intercontinental would not get the trip.

The *Racing Post* reported:

Ouija Board's connections were satisfied with second spot after a summer in which she missed several engagements due to injury and was almost retired.

Trainer Ed Dunlop said: 'She ran a great race. The winner was drawn one and had much more speed than us – ours needs 1½ miles. She ran a phenomenal race for a filly who nearly retired mid-season.'

Bailey said: 'I can't fault her – she ran a good race. I got a good run early and was only three

wide and that was exactly where I wanted to be. She made a nice run at the filly on the lead. I thought we would catch her. I thought Intercontinental would stop a little, but she did not. The other filly just ran too well.'

Hindsight is a great lens through which to view what might have been, and it is by no means certain that she would have won had Jerry kept closer to Intercontinental. We could still count our blessings, and the need to keep a sense of perspective was starkly brought home by the fate of Funfair, who was running prominently in the Mile later in the afternoon when he broke a leg and had to be destroyed. At least we still had our horse, and we felt desperate for the Thompsons, owners of the Cheveley Park Stud, and for their manager Chris Richardson.

Later that afternoon our disappointment was alleviated by having Baron George von Ullman join us at our table to celebrate his colt Shirocco winning the Breeders' Cup Turf in pulverising style.

By now Ouija Board was no longer my only horse in training. There were three, and Chess Board, Ouija Board's three-parts brother trained by Sir Mark Prescott, ran the same day as the Breeders' Cup at the somewhat more humble venue of Wolverhampton, in a median auction maiden stakes worth £3,438 to the winner. Not that Chess Board ever looked like delivering that sum to go with the £110,417 that Ouija Board earned

Ouija Board and Chris Hinson – front page news in Japan.

from coming second. 'Outpaced throughout', reported the form book gloomily, and he finished eleventh of twelve runners.

With four weeks between the Breeders' Cup and her next target, the Japan Cup, Ouija Board returned to Newmarket. She had come out of her Belmont exertions extremely well and took the flight to Tokyo in her stride, arriving twelve days before the race.

I had been to Japan once before on business nearly two decades earlier, and had been immediately struck, as all first-time visitors to that country are, by the extraordinary cultural differences from what we are used to. What might appear to the British an insignificant activity takes on serious meaning there. For example, while I would casually hand a British person my business card, in Japan this everyday transaction must be done holding the card in both hands, and it will be received in both hands, accompanied by a fair amount of bowing and appreciative noises from both parties. And your card must include your details in Japanese, so far as is practical. Japan is a complete man's world, a fact which was forcibly borne in on Cazzy and on Becky Dunlop during Ouija Board's first trip there. Both Cazzy and I had business cards printed up with English details on one side and Japanese on the other, and while I was merrily doling mine out to a steady stream of people, Cazzy hardly used any, as Japanese men were just not interested in being introduced to women. The Japanese were invariably courteous and friendly towards her, but as women in what strikes me as an extraordinarily misogynist society, she, Becky and Jane George, the International Racing Bureau's representative in Japan, just had to laugh about it. Both on this trip and on our return in 2006, Jane was a fantastic courier, guide, interpreter and friend in a country where the overseas visitor needs a considerable amount of assistance, both with

regard to the culture and the language and in more practical areas: it struck me as ironic that in a country famous for its development of high-tech electronic goods, neither my Blackberry nor my mobile phone seemed to work!

The racing authorities in Japan, like in Hong Kong, are exceptionally generous. An overseas owner taking a horse to the Breeders' Cup has to pay all expenses for his party, including his trainer, jockey and, crucially, his horse: flying a horse to Belmont Park and back costs in the region of £25,000. But both Japan and Hong Kong not only pay the expenses of visiting connections and their horses, but they lay on wonderfully generous parties and dinners during the days leading up to the international races. At the gala dinner before the Japan Cup, I was reluctantly persuaded to go up on the stage with Frankie Dettori and make our own contribution to the traditional drum-playing. Ouija Board's wondrous international career has brought me many new experiences, but few quite as strange as that.

Frankie's Japan Cup ride was Alkaased, whose trainer Luca Cumani had travelled over on his own and who spent a good deal of time with us, becoming affectionately known as 'The Spare Wop'.

Throughout the trip we were beautifully looked after. We were staying in the Century Hyatt Hotel, and John Wallis, whose brother Stephen runs Epsom Downs racecourse, is a senior figure in Hyatt and saw to it that we had a very good room. Stephen also arranged for us to have dinner with Chika Koga, boss of Hyatt Asia and a mad keen racing fan, at the New York Grill in the Park Hyatt – featured in the film *Lost in*

Translation – where we enjoyed a wonderful meal of the famous Kobe beef. Among the other guests were Teri Yoshida, owner of the Shadai Farm, Japan's most renowned stud, and his wife. We enjoyed getting to know them better, both in Japan and England.

Also memorable was a party thrown by Fusao Sekiguchi, who made his own grand entrance down his sweeping gold staircase. He invited me to come and inspect his special Buddha, and led me up a gilded spiral staircase (he adds more gold after each Group 1 victory) – other guests following in our wake, keen as mustard to see what was upstairs – to see an extraordinary statue of Buddha, about two feet tall, with a horse's head incorporated into the Buddha's head. This was Sekiguchi San's good luck charm, to bring the safe return of all horses in a race – he has racing interests all over the world, and his most famous horse has been Fusaichi Pegasus, who won the Kentucky Derby in 2000 – and he gave many of us miniatures of the statue: I now carry mine on my race-glasses.

Ouija Board was again accompanied by the familiar figures of Chris Hinson (who had flown over with her in the

Kieren Fallon and Chris Hinson familiarise Ouija Board with the huge paddock at Fuchu in advance of her big day (below), and (right) she finishes a close-up fifth as Alkaased (number 14) just beats Heart's Cry. Note, in Kieren's cap, the variation from the traditional Derby colours: in Japan the colour of each jockey's caps relates to the horse's draw position.

plane) and Robin Trevor-Jones, who like all visiting teams of grooms were given their own Japanese interpreter, and were soon experiencing the no-nonsense approach of the Japanese racing authorities. The filly was billeted at the quarantine station at Shiroi, two hours from Tokyo, and Robin and Chris were housed in small apartments directly over her box. This had the advantage that they were always on the spot, but the disadvantage that they were constantly at Ouija Board's beck and call, a sort of equine room service. Every night she considered 1 a.m. the right moment for a snack, and registered her order by kicking the door of her box until Chris, still in his nocturnal boxer shorts, had got out of bed and gone down to serve up half a bowl of feed and an apple – upon receiving which Ouija Board would become placid again and he climb the stairs and go back to bed.

Not only did the visiting grooms have to remain on the premises during their stay in Japan – and they could not even slip out for a quick drink, as foreigners were not served in the local bars – but they also had to surrender much of the basic equipment which they routinely took on Ouija Board's travels abroad, including the vet box which formed an essential part of Robin's baggage. Particularly galling for the filly herself was that she was denied her favourite extra-strong mints, and took a dim view of the lemon-flavoured Japanese sweets offered in their place. (Jockeys, no matter how famous they are, are locked up at the racecourse from the afternoon before the race.)

Fuchu is a stunning racecourse, one of its most engaging features being a pathway in a

107

garden behind the massive grandstand built in the shape, and with the contours, of the Derby course at Epsom, yet another example of the family name cropping up in places very far from home.

The national equine hero Deep Impact was not running in the Japan Cup, but there was none the less a very strong local challenge headed by Heart's Cry, who in the Arima Kinen later that month would be the very first horse to beat Deep Impact. Since it was first run in 1981, the Japan Cup has always attracted a strong overseas challenge, and the 2005 raiders included, in addition to Ouija Board and Alkaased, the 2004 Arc winner Bago (who had finished third in that race in 2005) and Clive Brittain's hardy warrior Warrsan.

We had no great expectation of victory – certainly this seemed a much tougher proposition on paper than the Filly and Mare Turf – and learning that Ouija Board was given as fifth favourite in the *Racing Post* before the race seemed a fair reflection of her chance.

In the event she ran another blinder, making headway approaching the straight, moving smoothly into third, and then going second with a quarter of a mile to go. Inside the final furlong she sustained a hefty bump from Heart's Cry, who was making rapid progress and just failed to sustain her run, eventually finishing a close-up fifth behind Alkaased and Frankie, who pipped Heart's Cry by a very short head (in the local parlance, a nose) and beat the track record into the bargain. Ouija Board in fifth was only about two lengths behind the winner. It would be stretching a point to suggest that the bump from

Heart's Cry cost Ouija Board the race, but it did her no favours at a crucial moment and without it she may well have finished third, since there was only a nose and a neck between the third-placed horse Zenno Rob Roy and Ouija Board in fifth. Yet again she had turned in a top-class effort, and we left Japan very happy.

The plan had always been for an Asian campaign in the autumn, and as soon as Ouija Board had indicated that she was still in fine fettle, she was flown down to Hong Kong to acclimatise at Sha Tin racecourse ahead of the massive Cathay Pacific-sponsored international race day there on 11 December, two weeks after the Japan Cup.

On the night of the Japan Cup a small group of us went to an Italian restaurant with a group of people which included Mark Player, who masterminds the Hong Kong International Races, and Ciaran Connolly, the senior handicapper in Hong Kong. Conversation naturally and rapidly turned to Ouija Board's Hong Kong prospects, and at this stage it had not been decided whether she would run in the Hong Kong Cup over ten furlongs or the Hong Kong Vase over twelve. There were strong arguments either way, but what finally swayed us was that in the shorter race the draw for stalls positions was more crucial, as the first bend comes up very quickly in a 1¼ mile race at Sha Tin, making it important to be sharply away in order to reach a favourable position. Ouija Board always tended to leave the stalls in her own time, and the extra distance would play more into her style of racing, allowing her more time to find the ideal place. So the Hong Kong Vase it would be.

A photo we could not resist having taken – at the restaurant named after my forebear Lord Stanley (later 15th Earl of Derby).

The next morning we flew back to England for ten days before setting off for Hong Kong – where upon arrival we behaved like most European visitors and rushed off to the shops, with Sam the shirtmaker, A-Man Hing Chong the tailor and Meyer the shoemaker heading the list of essential destinations. That Thursday evening we were generously invited by David Tang to use the China Club for dinner, and were joined by Peter, our friends Alex Appleby and Emma Sherrard, along with Emma's mother Sarah, Jimmy George of Tattersalls, husband of Jane, who had looked after us so well in Japan, and Agnieszka Szeluk (now Mrs Charles Butter).

Hong Kong, where East and West meet in unique fashion, is hardly less of a culture shock to the visitor than Japan, but the former colony carries specific family echoes for me. Stanley Harbour, on the southern coast of the island, is named after my ancestor the 15th Earl, who has the distinction of serving in the Cabinet both as a Tory foreign secretary and later as a Liberal colonial secretary, and Murray House at Stanley Harbour was the venue, two days before the races, for the gala party, on leaving which we were highly amused to find ourselves walking by a restaurant named 'Lord Stanley at the Curry Pot'!

Over the last few years the ever-enterprising Hong Kong Jockey Club has been determinedly increasing the status of its glittering international race day in December, where the four races which now attract the cream of overseas challengers are the Hong Kong Vase, Hong Kong Cup, Hong Kong Mile and Hong Kong Sprint. All four big races now enjoy Group 1 status, and the big day is more and more a magnet for the world's very best racehorses. Eager to maintain the status of the occasion, the Hong Kong Jockey Club matches the generosity of the Japanese Racing Association towards visiting horses and connections. They provide: for the owner and trainer, two Business Class return air tickets each and accommodation in the Grand Hyatt Hotel; for the jockey a similar package; for the horse, all shipment costs plus stabling, bedding, fodder and so on; and for the groom, air ticket plus hotel accommodation near Sha Tin racecourse, which is situated in the New Territories on the mainland. (A special vote of thanks goes to a wonderful lady named Symphorosa So, who has looked after our arrangements superbly on our three trips to Hong Kong with Ouija Board, and to the Wallis family, who once again ensured that we had a very comfortable stay in the Grand Hyatt – though the latter part of our stay was disrupted by preparations for the imminent meeting of the World Trade Organisation, with roads being closed as the centre of Hong Kong was closed off, and traffic restrictions made getting around rather awkward.)

The Hong Kong Vase attracted a

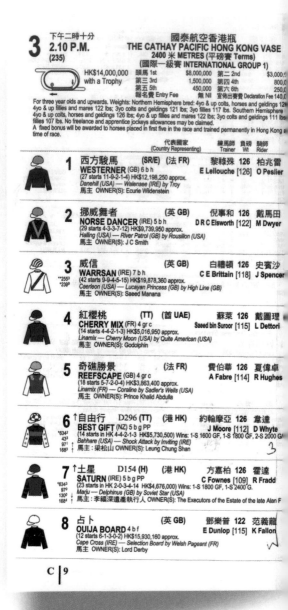

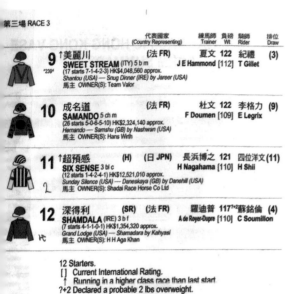

第三場 RACE 3

			代表國家 (Country Representing)	練馬師 Trainer	負磅 Wt	騎師 Rider	排位 Draw

9 ↑美麗川
SWEET STREAM (ITY) 5 b m   (法 FR)   夏文 122   紀禮 (3)
239 (17 starts 7-1-4-2-3) HK$4,048,560 approx.   J E Hammond [112]   T Gillet
Shantou (USA) — Snug Dinner (IRE) by Jareer (USA)
馬主 OWNER(S): Team Valor

10 成名道
SAMANDO 5 ch m   (法 FR)   杜文 122   李格力 (9)
(26 starts 5-0-6-5-10) HK$2,324,140 approx.   F Doumen [109]   E Legrix
Hernando — Samshu (GB) by Nashwan (USA)
馬主 OWNER(S): Hans Wirth

11 ↑超預感
SIX SENSE 3 b c   (H)   (日 JPN)   長浜博之 121   四位洋文 (11)
(12 starts 1-4-2-4-1) HK$12,521,010 approx.   H Nagahama [110]   H Shii
Sunday Silence (USA) — Daneskaya (GB) by Danehill (USA)
馬主 OWNER(S): Shadai Race Horse Co Ltd

12 深得利
SHAMDALA (IRE) 3 b f   (SR)   (法 FR)   羅迪普 117?+2 蘇銘倫 (4)
(7 starts 4-1-1-0-1) HK$1,354,320 approx.   A de Royer-Dupre [110]   C Soumillon
Grand Lodge (USA) — Shamadara by Kahyasi
馬主 OWNER(S): H H Aga Khan

12 Starters.
[]   Current International Rating.
↑   Running in a higher class race than last start
?+2 Declared a probable 2 lbs overweight.

CATHAY PACIFIC
國泰航空公司

Standard Time: 2.28.8

1st	2nd	3rd	4th	Finishing Time
stances				
in $	Quinella $		Tierce $	Trio $
uinella Place	(1st & 2nd) $	(1st & 3rd) $		(2nd & 3rd) $
ace	(1st) $	(2nd) $		(3rd) $
uble $				

C | 10

characteristically top-class field, but I was surprised that Westerner, owned by Alec Wildenstein, was favourite: he was a brilliant stayer who had won the Ascot Gold Cup at York and then finished runner-up to Hurricane Run in the Arc, but I thought a mile and a half round Sha Tin on what would be firmish ground would not be up his street at all. When people asked about our chances, I always pointed out that he was hot favourite, but privately I thought that we would at least beat him. The rest of the field included Shamdala, Cherry Mix, Samando, Reefscape and Sweet Stream from France, and Cherry Mix, Warrsan and Norse Dancer from England.

In the paddock before the race we were discussing tactics with Kieren when we were surprised to be suddenly joined by Sam the Tailor, who slid in and attached himself to our party, promising Kieren that if he were to win on Ouija Board he would make him a suit!

The race was remarkable. Kieren got Ouija Board to break nicely, and coming past the stands first time round she was settled in behind. But going down the back straight she lost her place, going further and further back in the field to the point where she was soon plumb last, and there was a wall of horses in front of her. Not only did she have an immense amount of ground to make up, she had no way of getting through to mount her challenge. I muttered in disbelief to Cazzy and Peter, 'What is Kieren up to?' – and at the end of the back straight her position looked hopeless. Peter shrugged, 'I'm sorry, but that's it', and I could not disagree.

She was still last as the field came round the

The Hong Kong Vase, 2005: Ouija Board surges clear – and another trophy for her ecstatic owner.

final bend, and then, as they emerged from it, in an instant the race was transformed. I have watched the film of this race over and over, and still cannot see where the gap came from. But come it did, and Ouija Board shot straight through at the beginning of the straight and was away, putting instant daylight between herself and her rivals and scorching home by 2¾ lengths from Sixth Sense. Westerner finished fifth.

Kieren had given our filly a ride of pure genius, and left no one in doubt as to the status of his partner: 'I've ridden some seriously good fillies like Bosra Sham and Islington,' he told the press, 'and on this evidence she must be right up there with them. The one thing which went wrong was that I had to take her back in the early stages, but I knew if I didn't get her settled she definitely wouldn't finish. This filly has a lot of speed and I was confident she would accelerate if the splits came.'

After the elaborate presentation ceremony – during which the indefatigable Sam the Tailor managed to infiltrate himself onto the rostrum before being ejected by Mark Player, and then found his way back before being thrown off again! – we

brought the Vase itself back to our lunch table, having to run the gauntlet of some extremely po-faced security guards who could not enter into the spirit of the moment at all. The guards were very concerned when I carried the Vase off in the opposite direction for an interview with Jim McGrath. But having come so far for this wonderful trophy, I was not minded to let it out of my grasp if I could help it.

(My mother and stepfather Bill, not with us on this occasion, had invested in Sky Television in order to see the race, as they felt they could not impose upon friends to watch at 6.20 a.m. in Britain. Having been brought up in a racing family, my mother was over the moon and rang Simon Sherrard to say: 'Quick! Put on the television. Ouija has won and your wife and daughter [Sarah and Emma] are up on the rostrum with Teddy and Cazzy!' – to be met with the sleepy response, 'Rosie, it's 6.30 a.m.!' 'So what?', my mother replied: 'You're obviously not a racing man!')

Our joy was shared by the racing community at home. On the day after the race Peter Thomas wrote in the *Racing Post*:

Yesterday's barnstorming victory in the Cathay Pacific Hong Kong Vase finally confirmed to us that although Dunlop may not be a deity, he can still work a minor miracle, and that contrary to popular belief, there is a God up there somewhere, as he still occasionally finds time to smile on the righteous.

We've all seen too many good horses packed

Team Ouija Board with their heroine after the Hong Kong Vase: left to right, Peter Stanley, Robin Trevor-Jones, Chris Hinson, Cazzy and Becky Dunlop.

in those wiggly bits of polystyrene throughout their racing careers, and then whisked off to the rogering sheds before they're metaphorically out of short trousers, so Lord Derby could have escaped with barely a murmur of public dissent if he'd done the sensible thing and drawn stumps with Ouija Board once she'd clouted two Classics and a Breeders' Cup to the boundary last year.

If he'd retired his pride and joy when she was crocked at the start of this season, or when she was crocked in the lead-up to York, we might even have said he was eminently wise, and probably he would have been. But, mercifully, the sportsman's instinct overrode all considerations of common sense, and the potty peer's flight of fancy has been rewarded with so much foreign currency that the staff at his local post office must be dreading him coming in to change it up.

Of course, it's nice that the Derbys won't have to lay off the butler after all, and that Mrs D. will be able to afford a new outfit at last, but the main thing is that we've seen the vindication of a decision based on a bold competitive instinct and an unwavering faith in a very capable trainer, who himself never lost faith in the ability of his staff to revitalise a brilliant but fragile racehorse.

I appreciated that endorsement, though I'm not sure how to react to being called 'the potty peer'!

The following Thursday, David Ashforth's *Post* piece contained a fascinating analysis of the sectional times:

How many racefans watching the Hong Kong Vase at Sha Tin last Sunday were asking Kieren Fallon what he was doing loitering at the back on Ouija Board? As one of my pet hates is jockeys who sit a long way off a slow pace – a practice I associate with incompetence or non-trying, with occasional mitigation for unavoidable circumstances – I confess that I was one of those racefans.

Kieren, partly because he was 13,400 miles away, and partly because he can ride rather better than me, wasn't listening, but provided a pretty convincing answer when he sent Ouija Board streaking through a gap to breathtaking victory. How did it happen?

It looked a slow early pace, and the sectional timings confirm that it was a slow pace. In 2003, when Vallee Enchantee won in 2.28.2, the first 400 metres were covered in 25.8 seconds. Last year, in a race regarded as notably slow, won by Phoenix Reach in a relatively pedestrian 2.29.8, the opening fraction was 26.5. This year, it was even slower, 26.6 – and there was Fallon, at the back of it.

He wasn't there entirely by choice – Fallon reported that he would have preferred to be closer to the pace, but his priority was to get Ouija Board settled.

Last year, each successive fraction was faster than the previous one, with closing fractions of 23.5 and 23.1 seconds. This year, on the way to Ouija Board's winning time of 2.28.9, it was a case of slow, quick, slow, slow then quicker. The most striking 400 metres was the second one, timed at 24.1 seconds – compare that with a time of 26 seconds last year, and 24.7 seconds in a faster race in 2003.

So some pace was injected during the first

third of the race, before settling back to two matching fractions of 25.4 seconds, followed by closing fractions of 24.0 and 23.4 – compared with 23.1 last year.

However you interpret the figures, the sight of Ouija Board making ground, nosing through a gap, and running away from her rivals, was gripping and heartwarming ...

For me the Hong Kong Vase was an enormously significant result. Ouija Board had won a Group 1 race as a four-year-old, to complement her three Group 1 successes the previous year; she had beaten colts at Group 1 level for the first time; she had overcome the desperately disheartening setback of the York injury; and she had shown herself to be better than ever, a filly who could take on the best in the world and – sometimes – beat them.

The Ouija Board Debating Society had reconvened the day before the Vase in a magnificent 56-foot long boat named *Hard Times* – a sort of modern take on the traditional Chinese junk, but without the sails – moored at the AMC Marina Club at Aberdeen and co-owned by Rob Appleby and his wife Alex, old friends of Cazzy's. The only subject on the agenda was whether to continue campaigning Ouija Board into 2006.

Mindful above all of Ouija Board's towering importance in the future of Stanley House Stud, Peter thought the time had come to send Ouija Board off to the paddocks and be mated to Sadler's Wells. But her 2005 programme had been so interrupted that Ed and I felt that, assuming she came through the Hong Kong race unscathed, we would consider going to Nad Al Sheba on Dubai World Cup day in March for the Sheema Classic, a massively valuable race over 1½ miles which seemed to suit our filly down to the ground. There was even talk of running her in Dubai and then having her covered, but the timing made such a plan very complicated and risky. If we went to Dubai we would leave open the option of carrying on with her later in 2006, but on the basis of 'One race at a time', we knew that we had to see first how she performed at Sha Tin.

Which is why I said to Ed after the Hong Kong Vase: 'You've got yourself a horse in training for next year.'

Meanwhile Ouija Board remained, along with Court Masterpiece, the star incumbent of Gainsborough Stables. Plans to give her a long lay-off were shelved, as she was so well in herself that the idea of running her in the Sheema Classic began to exert a magnetic appeal. So she was kept on the go during the early months of the year, and on 2 March was in the news again when she went to work on the new all-weather course at Kempton Park, thus providing the unusual spectacle of a Flat horse in training performing the opening ceremony for the new track. She was due to be ridden

Photo opportunity at Kempton Park: Jason Tate and Ouija Board christen the new all-weather surface.

in this high-profile work by Jamie Spencer, who had been on board when she scored her first victory at Yarmouth but also that desperate afternoon at York. Then word came that Jamie would not make it to Kempton Park as his wife Emma had gone into hospital and was about to give birth to their first child – so naturally his presence was required there.

We found a ready replacement for Jamie in Jason Tate, former jockey and one of the best work riders in Newmarket, who at very short notice came down to ride her, thereby commencing a relationship which was to last through the year and was to take Jason to places

he might not have anticipated visiting. The sight of one of the world's great racehorses travelling smoothly round the new circuit provided Kempton with the ideal photo-call, and our mare (as by then she had become, as a filly becomes a mare upon turning five) with a fresh pasture on which to continue her build-up towards Dubai. (It is worth noting that until this point all Ouija Board's serious work at home had been on artificial all-weather services. It was not until she was five years old that she ever worked on Newmarket's turf gallops.)

Since Ouija Board's 2005 season had in effect begun with the Princess Royal Stakes at Newmarket in October, the approach to the Sheema Classic felt like coming to the end of that campaign, rather than the start of a new season, and the prospect of exchanging the chill of Newmarket in early spring for the heat of Dubai triggered some imaginative thinking at Gainsborough Stables.

When in Tokyo for the Japan Cup, Chris Hinson and Ed had been very impressed by the standard of stabling which Ouija Board had enjoyed, in particular the infra-red lamps which heated her box, and it was decided to fit her box at home with similar lamps, to minimise how she would react to the difference between temperatures in Newmarket and Dubai. They went further, fitting Ouija Board with a thick and snug hood to keep her warm when she went out onto the Heath, and she took to wearing four rugs. It is the accumulation of such apparently small attentions to detail which turns a good training operation into a great one, and throughout her career Ouija Board could not

Chris Hinson and 'Mother' snugly protected from the Newmarket chill – and (right) after her post-shower roll in Dubai.

have been in better hands.

We decided to take all three children out of school – the term was all but over anyway – and booked into Dar Al Masyaf, one of three amazing hotels disposed over a series of islands, each hotel having no central area but consisting of a series of Arab-style courtyards, around which are some ten rooms. The mode of transport between different parts of the hotel is, as appropriate, golf buggy or electric boat. Ed and Becky brought their three girls – Emily, Rose and Martha – and their nanny Debbie, and we knew that, win or lose at Nad Al Sheba, we would have a memorable family holiday. (Also with us were my mother, in the week of her birthday, and her sister my aunt Bridget Hanbury and Bridget's husband Christopher, chairman of the Hurlingham Polo Association – so a day at Dubai's polo ground was firmly on the agenda.)

Everything about Dubai – racing and otherwise – is immaculately organised, and the generosity of the Dubai Racing Club towards visiting connections and horses rivals that of Japan or Hong Kong. Particularly spectacular was the Party in the Desert a couple of days before the World Cup. In the early evening visitors are bussed out to the desert, where at a venue arranged like a Bedouin camp they are served a wonderful variety of food and drink, and can engage in a wide variety of activities, including camel riding. As darkness falls the place becomes even more magical, and Hetty and the three Dunlop girls were in seventh heaven with having henna tattoos applied, while our boys Edward and Oliver especially liked the falcons.

We were invited by Frankie and Catherine

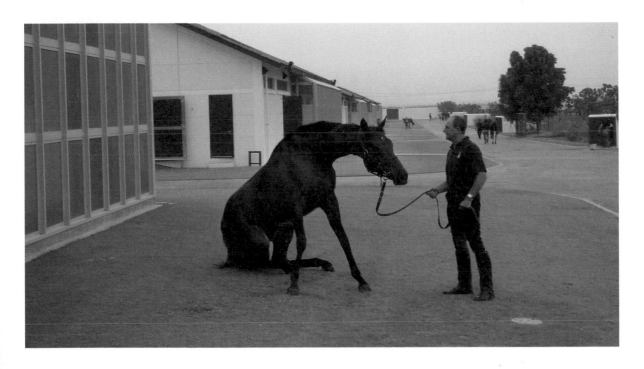

Our children and the Dunlop children, and our nanny Carole Dowson, enjoyed themselves to the full in Dubai!

Dettori to join them in the exclusive inner section next to the tables put aside for the party of Sheikh Mohammed, whose immense efforts to put Dubai on the world racing map have been so brilliantly successful. When the Sheikh and his wife Princess Haya arrived, attended by a huge retinue of men wearing the dish-dash – the traditional white robe – I was anxious to thank our host in person, and equally anxious to follow the correct protocol when doing so. The Dunlops advised that I simply had to jostle my way through the dish-dashed retinue to get to the Sheikh, and somewhat uneasily Cazzy and I followed their advice, forcing our way up to him just as the astonishing firework display was getting under way. I said to Sheikh Mohammed what an honour it was to have a daughter of Cape Cross good enough to be

invited to race in Dubai, and when he expressed himself delighted that his stallion had produced such a mare I recalled that moment at Epsom just after the 2004 Oaks, when behind the massed photographers snapping away at the winner I could see the lone figure of Sheikh Mohammed, gazing in admiration at a filly who, his expert eye was telling him, was something very special.

On the eve of Dubai World Cup day Diana Cooper, a key member of the Godolphin staff, called on Princess Haya's behalf to invite us to a barbecue that evening at the Sheikh's palace on the beach. There were only about sixteen guests, plus the Godolphin team – about twenty-four people in all – and I found Princess Haya (who earlier in the day had presented the trophy for the polo competition) utterly charming, with the most captivating smile. Cazzy particularly enjoyed having a long discussion with her about equestrianism, in which the Princess, as President of the International Equestrian Federation, is now such an important figure.

We had not expected Sheikh Mohammed himself to appear but at about 9.30 he did, and we saw at first hand the Sheikh's marvellous sense of humour, rarely glimpsed at his racecourse appearances in Britain. The food and wines were fabulous, and the party finished a great deal later than we had anticipated at about 1.30.

A few hours later my usual pre-race run took me along the shore, but the midday heat was so intense that I had to stop at a hotel in order to take on water. The daytime temperature in Dubai demands that the races take place in the cool of the evening, and, feeling slightly uneasy in the light of what had happened when we had first taken all three children to watch Ouija Board in action in the Yorkshire Oaks, we set off for the Nad Al Sheba racecourse in time to ensure that we would be there to see Ed's colt Court Masterpiece run in the Godolphin Mile, the first race on the programme, but not too early, as we did not want to subject the children to too long an evening.

It was when Court Masterpiece's jockey walked into the parade ring that Cazzy and I started to feel very uneasy. Kieren Fallon, who had not ridden in a race since the day of the Hong Kong Vase three months earlier, had been flown out specifically to ride both Ed's Dubai runners, but the jockey striding across in the familiar Maktoum al Maktoum colours was not walking like Kieren. It was not Kieren. It was Michael Kinane. What on earth had happened? Where was our jockey?

After the race – in which Court Masterpiece finished a never-dangerous sixth behind Utopia – we discovered that Kieren was stuck in traffic, and the team hastily convened in order to discuss what to do. Someone suggested substituting Frankie there and then – he did not have a ride in the race – but I could not jock off someone who had ridden such a brilliant race on Ouija Board last time out.

We decided to stick with Kieren, though we were not impressed to hear that he had left at the same time as us from the same hotel, as he needed to be at the racecourse before us. Shortly before our race we went down to the weighing room, and Cazzy instantly spotted an ominous sight: the lucky white button on the Derby silks had not been done up! Superstition may be irrational, but it has played its part in most people's racing lives, and to see the greatest instance of a family lucky charm not engaged before one of Ouija Board's biggest moments was an extremely gloomy omen. Cazzy pointed out the omission to Kieren and he did up the white button without apparently sharing our concern for the omens, but the damage had been done: our optimism had been draining away since first seeing Michael Kinane in the Court Masterpiece colours, and now there was precious little left.

Immediately before the Sheema Classic – with a prize fund of $5 million the richest turf race in the world – there was a great firework display, very spectacular but not ideal for settling a horse! To our relief, Robin and Chris assured us that

Ouija Board seemed to have paid very little attention, and had not turned a hair.

The race itself sent our gloom to new depths, for Ouija Board never gave us a single moment when we could think she was going to win. For too long she seemed stuck in the middle of the field, and when Kieren did attempt a forward move about half a mile out, then brought her wide a furlong later, she made little progress and never offered the slightest suggestion that she might be involved in the shake-up. She finished fourth, nine lengths behind the winner Heart's Cry (to whom she had been much closer in the Japan Cup), with Collier Hill, the globe-totting gelding trained in Yorkshire by Alan Swinbank, second, and Falstaff from South Africa third. One place behind Ouija Board came Alexander Goldrun.

Perhaps it is politic to leave the post-mortem to·the words of *Racing Post* reporter Lee Mottershead two days later:

Ed Dunlop has made clear his disappointment with 'an unsatisfactory race in every respect' for his superstar mare Ouija Board, who was yesterday reported in excellent shape after her hugely frustrating reappearance run under Kieren Fallon in the Dubai Sheema Classic at Nad Al Sheba on Saturday.

Dunlop, who had produced 2004 Horse of the Year Ouija Board in peak condition for her first start since landing the Hong Kong Vase in December, was left to reflect on what might have been after Lord Derby's Breeders' Cup winner was set what proved an impossible task in the $5 million feature.

Making a point of praising winning rider Christophe Lemaire for executing 'the sort of ride one expects from a top jockey in a tactical contest', Dunlop distanced himself from Fallon's post-race assertion that pre-race fireworks were to blame for the dual Classic heroine's below-par performance.

Fallon failed to arrive at Nad Al Sheba in time to partner the Dunlop-trained Court Masterpiece in the opening Godolphin Mile and, as a result, was having his first ride for three months when teaming up with 9-4 favourite Ouija Board.

The Ballydoyle stable jockey, who had last been in competitive action when riding his Nad Al Sheba mount in Hong Kong on December 11, settled her in mid-division while Lemaire dictated a slow pace on Heart's Cry. Brought wide into the straight, Ouija Board made significant inroads in the closing stages, but at no point threatened to land a blow.

Commenting on Ouija Board's Dubai experience, Dunlop – who is now considering running the five-year-old in either the Queen Elizabeth II Cup at Sha Tin next month or in May's Singapore Airlines International Cup – said: 'I know it was suggested by some that she was unsettled by the noise of the fireworks, but that theory isn't in the least valid in my opinion. The fact that she lost not a bit of weight as a result of her exertions before or during the race rather makes that clear. She was not affected by the fireworks.

'I made a statement before Dubai saying she would have a long holiday after the Sheema Classic, but that is now not a certainty. As a result of what happened, she has not had a hard race

and we might well now consider targets in Hong Kong and Singapore for her. We haven't decided about that yet, but what we do know is that she will have a European campaign this autumn.'

Confirming that Godolphin Mile sixth Court Masterpiece would also be campaigned back in Europe, Dunlop added: 'The problems Ouija Board encountered were entirely connected to the race itself, how it was run and, more specifically, how it panned out for her. For Ouija Board, it was an unsatisfactory race in every respect.

No need to describe the mood as jockey, trainer and owner conduct the post-mortem after the Sheema Classic.

'It was very slowly run and the first three through the race remained the first three at the

end of the race. What we saw was a perfectly executed ride by an extremely good young French jockey, who produced the sort of ride one expects from a top jockey in a tactical contest.'

Kieren could offer no satisfactory explanation beyond the effect of the fireworks, and in the end we just wanted to forget the race and look back on the generosity of the Maktoums in providing us with such a memorable few days. There were yet more memorable Dubai days to come after the races were over, as we stayed out there for our family holiday, and the children adored every moment, being driven over the sand dunes, marvelling at the sinuous skills of belly dancers, more falcons and henna tattoos, and even persuading their father to ride on a camel!

The intention had been to consider the Sheema Classic as the final race of Ouija Board's current term and give her a proper break before coming back for some of the big middle-distance races of the summer, with a view very strongly on another international autumn campaign. But the outcome of the Sheema Classic was so deeply unsatisfactory that we thought we would try to get the taste of it out of our mouths by taking her to Hong Kong again in late April, this time for the Audemars Piquet Queen Elizabeth II Cup over 1¼ miles.

Chris Hinson, Ouija Board's usual work rider and companion on her earlier long-haul trips, could not be spared from early-season duties in Newmarket to make the Hong Kong trip with his beloved mare, whom he and everyone else close to her now affectionately addressed as 'Mother'. So on this occasion her attendants were Jason

Robin Trevor-Jones stops the Newmarket traffic for Ouija Board and Frankie.

Tate and Robin Trevor-Jones, and they were billeted close to the quarantine barn at Sha Tin. (It is a tribute to their skills – and to Chris, who had accompanied Ouija Board to Hong Kong the previous December – that before both her races at Sha Tin our filly was named Best Turned Out. To have maintained her bloom after she had travelled so far from a cold Newmarket was some achievement.)

Ed arrived in Hong Kong on the Thursday, three days before the race, and when Becky and I arrived in Hong Kong on the Friday lunchtime we went straight to the track from the airport to see Ouija Board, who looked in magnificent shape after her long journey. What makes a racehorse a good international traveller is mostly a question of temperament, but whatever the magic ingredient, our mare had it by the bucket-load. By now her intercontinental travel had already taken her to Texas, New York and Japan as well as the first visit to Hong Kong, and she had hardly turned a hair. Brian Taylor, her flying groom on these and subsequent trips, attributes the ease with which she travels simply to that unflappable temperament – 'She's just perfect' – and that Friday at the Sha Tin quarantine barn she looked in great shape.

When we arrived at the Grand Hyatt Hotel I immediately noticed a crowd of about fifty people standing around outside the lobby entrance, including the general manager Gordon Fuller. 'Who's arriving?', I asked Gordon – only to receive the answer, 'You are!' Apparently the Hyatt staff had won so much money on Ouija Board in the Hong Kong Vase in December that

The Audemars Piquet Queen Elizabeth II Cup, 2006: Ouija Board just fails to catch Irridescence (sheepskin noseband) and Best Gift.

the hotel's holiday rota was bursting at the seams for weeks afterwards, and the gratitude of the management for their good fortune was reflected in the huge and magnificent suite of rooms, high above the harbour and commanding a magnificent view, which we had been allotted. Cazzy arrived in time for lunch on Saturday and Peter and Frances later that afternoon, and in the evening ate at a characterless Chinese restaurant – complete with bright strip lighting and lino floors – which had been recommended by one of Ed's owners and was thereafter known to our party as 'Ed's Diner'. Having stocked up with

decent wine from a vintner across the road, we left ordering of the food to the management, and could scarcely cope with course after course of local dishes being delivered to our table, which I have to say I found too Chinese for a western palate. Ed came in for a good deal of stick about directing us to this restaurant, and when next morning there were a fair few thick heads and upset stomachs in our party we were inclined to blame the food – though Ed insists that these ailments were odds on to have been related to the quantity of wine taken on board!

That the 2006 Queen Elizabeth II Cup – in which Frankie was reunited with Ouija Board – was being run on 23 April, St George's Day, was highly appropriate, as the race had been founded by the Queen during a visit to Hong Kong in 1975. But the timing caused us a problem, as we had accepted to go to the service at St George's Chapel at Windsor Castle to mark Her Majesty's eightieth birthday, and had to send belated apologies. We had hoped to be able to report that our absence from that very special royal occasion had at least been compensated with success in the race named after The Queen, but sadly that was not to be.

Ouija Board broke slowly yet again and settled in nicely, but then going down the back straight got shuffled towards the rear by a tiring horse, and by the home turn was tenth of the thirteen runners, her chance forlorn. Halfway up the straight Frankie switched her to the outside and she sprouted wings, maintaining a mighty surge throughout the final furlong. But Irridescence – trained in South Africa by Mike de Kock – and Best Gift were already engaged in slogging out a stirring finish, and Ouija Board arrived on the scene a fraction of a second too late. Irridescence beat Best Gift a head, with our mare a short head back in third. It had been incredibly close.

Frankie was cross and upset when he dismounted, banging his helmet down in frustration, and was convinced that but for those traffic problems going down the back she would have won. Watching a replay of the race it was hard not to agree with him, but what was important was that Ouija Board had run another very brave race, and had come out of it fresh.

For years Cazzy had been busy planning a major fund-raising event at the Royal Albert Hall to benefit the National Society for the Protection of Cruelty to Children – a Dream Auction, billed as 'The Night that Dreams are Made of' and aiming to raise enough money to fund the NSPCC's ground-breaking new website for abused children – www.there4me.com – for a period of at least ten years.

Cazzy was co-chairman of this major fund-raising initiative, at the centre of which was the Dream Auction itself, offering lots containing a strong 'money-can't buy' element: these included such extraordinarily valuable lots as a new Bugatti Veyron 16.4, which accelerates from 0 to 100 kilometres an hour in 2.5 seconds, and an opportunity to record your own demo track with professional musicians at Abbey Road Studios.

As long-time supporters of the NSPCC we were keen to donate a lot in this auction, and came up with the idea of offering a half share in the three-quarters sister to Ouija Board – by Cape Cross out of Cruinn A Bhord – who had been born in 2005. The filly, named Mischief Lady, would go into training with Ed and, barring setbacks, embark on her racing career in 2007. Others in the racing world added extra value to the lot (including attendance at major race meetings and a tour of the Coolmore Stud, and, at the end of the filly's career, an oil painting of her given by the leading equestrian artist Katie O'Sullivan), and we were hopeful that it would attract lively interest, then amazed and so grateful when it went to the Triermore Stud in County Meath for no less than £350,000 – which made Mischief Lady worth £700,000 – on paper rather than in reality, so this was a wonderfully generous donation to the charity. In total the event raised £5½ million, a record for any similar occasion at the Albert Hall and more than double the amount achieved by any other NSPCC fund-raiser.

Meanwhile Mischief Lady's distinguished three-parts sister had returned from Dubai fit and well. Ed had initially thought that she now deserved a long holiday, with time in the paddock every day, along with sessions in the horse-walker and ice spa, winding her down towards a well-deserved period of rest. 'But she kept defying us,' he recalls: she was bursting with health and keen for another outing, so it was decided to aim her at the Coronation Cup and then give her a break. All being well, we wanted her to be primed for an autumn campaign, a plan which too much racing at the highest level through the summer could scupper. With the exception of the Group 3 Princess Royal Stakes, her last twelve races had been at Group 1 level, and for a five-year-old mare to return a consistent level of form at such heights was quite extraordinary.

But her advancing years had given her some quirks, not least that she seemed, at home, to be getting lazier and lazier in her work, and when she spotted Ed waiting at the end of the gallop she would deduce that she'd done her bit and pull up. Many of those closest to her remarked how she had become aware of how good she was and was minded to save herself for the special occasions on the racecourse, and the growing foibles on the home gallops just added to her charm. 'She loved people,' says Chris Hinson, 'and she knew she was the queen' – which reminds me how Pat Cronin at the Stanley House Stud has long referred to Ouija Board as

'The Queen of Utopia'.

Having been denied a midsummer campaign in 2005 by the York injury, we were keen to see Ouija Board run in as many of the major domestic middle-distance championship races as possible. Ed was inclined to go straight to Royal Ascot, where the Prince of Wales's Stakes on the second day of the meeting or the Hardwicke Stakes later in the week were her two possible targets, but I was in favour of going first for the Coronation Cup at Epsom. First run in 1902 to mark the coronation of Edward VII, this is the first middle-distance Group 1 race of the season for the best older horses (it is confined to four-year-olds and over), and usually sees the reappearance of a small but highly select group of horses who have been making their mark at the highest level. Run nowadays on Oaks Day, the day before the Derby, it has tended to get less attention than it deserves, and seemed to me to be just the sort of contest which Ouija Board should be going for. Furthermore, I was attracted to the idea of running her again at Epsom, scene of the Oaks triumph which had catapulted her into the history books and, of course, a track with a very strong association with my family.

By now I was getting used to – and, to be honest, rather enjoying – the limelight into which Ouija Board had brought me, and sharing the ups and downs of her career with our team, her ever-expanding fan club (who were keeping up a steady stream of letters, cards and mints to the yard), the press and the wider racing community has been one of the most appealing aspects of the

The Coronation Cup, 2006: Ouija Board and Frankie have to give best to Christophe Soumillon and Shirocco.

whole story. Several journalists, doubtless scarred by encounters with more remote owners, had taken to characterising me as a sort of acceptable (and occasionally potty!) face of the aristocracy, and the weekend before the Epsom meeting I was particularly amused by a small piece in the *Sunday Mirror* by Alastair Down, under the headline 'ALL HAIL TOP TOFF TEDDY':

Teddy Derby, as unstuffy an aristo as you will meet, is not short of a fiver but, realising a filly like Ouija Board comes along once in a couple of generations, he is still racing her at five rather than packing her off to the paddock to make a fortune. Nine out of ten would have gone for the money.

Derby, who has a small boy's enthusiasm for Ouija Board's racing adventure, is on the board of more charities than you can shake a stick at, and the fearless way he has globetrotted has been a much appreciated hand-out for racing fans.

Even by the historic standards of the Coronation Cup, the 2006 renewal was vintage, as Ouija Board's five opponents included Baron George von Ullman's tremendous horse Shirocco, who had won the Breeders' Cup Turf at Belmont Park the previous autumn after finishing third to

Hurricane Run in the Arc. No wonder the *Racing Post* page previewing the race, mindful that coverage of the Oaks that day might be getting more space, was headlined: 'YOU CALL THIS THE SUPPORT ACT?' The story began:

Aperitifs do not come more delicious than this.

For some, the race before the Oaks is the most mouth-watering contest of the week.

Two of the world's finest middle-distance Thoroughbreds, one, Shirocco, trained by the greatest of all French trainers, the other, Ouija Board, an English sweetheart chasing a second historic Epsom triumph. Truly, this is a Coronation Cup to savour.

Enforcer, Ace, Notable Guest and Something Exciting were the other four runners, but early in straight it was obvious that the race lay between Shirocco and Ouija Board. Shirocco, a horse of immense presence and power, had taken the lead at Tattenham Corner and shaken off the challenge of Ace – then Frankie got down to work with a vengeance and tried to join issue. While she managed to get as close to Shirocco as a neck, he was impossible to pass that day, and try as she might she could not peg him back. Close home Frankie accepted the situation and eased her down to finish 1¾ lengths adrift. No wonder the *Racing Post* said that she had run 'another blinder', adding: 'A stronger pace would have suited, but that's not to say she would have beaten Shirocco under any circumstances.' It should also be remembered that the ground was softer than we would have liked, and Ouija Board was not able to show her usual devastating turn of foot.

Ouija Board came out of the race as fresh as a daisy, and we turned our attention to Royal Ascot, less than three weeks away.

Debating time again. Ed, Peter, Cazzy and I pondered long and hard over whether to go for the Prince of Wales's Stakes or the Hardwicke, the former a Group 1 race over 1¼ miles, the latter a Group 2 over 1½ miles. Peter was strongly in favour of the Prince of Wales, as in his view Ouija Board was essentially a 10-12 furlong horse, and for him it would be a greater achievement to run third in a very high-class Royal Ascot race than win the Group 2. Certainly, given the likely opposition and the fact that I for one had no worries over Ouija Board's stamina, the Hardwicke looked the easier proposition, and Ed pointed out that if, like any owner, I harboured dreams of leading in a Royal Ascot winner, the Hardwicke provided the more likely opportunity. But we had never gone for the easy option with Ouija Board, and the more I thought about it, the more I wanted to take on the very best ten-furlong horses at the highest level.

After its year away at York while the architecturally magnificent new grandstand at Ascot was being built, the Royal Meeting returned home in 2006. The strict Royal Ascot dress code emphatically ruled out superstitiously wearing my usual race-day clothes – except for the green tie – but both Cazzy and Becky looked resplendent in their outfits. Cazzy's unimpeachable logic was that 'If the Queen has spent £200 million building that new stand, the least I can do is dress to fit the occasion.' But I did not approve of the change of outfit, and was vocal in delivering my opinion.

We stayed at Bagshot with The Earl and Countess of Wessex, and drove over to Ascot from there and watched the Royal Procession. The Queen's party included many people from the racing industry, and most importantly The Prince of Wales, who was due to make the presentation following the race run in his name (though originally founded to honour Queen Victoria's son Bertie, later Edward VII, when he was Prince of Wales). I said to him that I did not dare to hope that I would be collecting the trophy from him later in the afternoon.

The Wednesday of Royal Ascot 2006 turned out to be a memorable day for Ouija Board's groom Pat Evens in more ways than one. She had arrived at Ascot racecourse with her charge and with travelling head lad Robin Trevor-Jones early that morning, having spent the journey from Newmarket sitting on an upturned bucket in the horse box close to Ouija Board's head, all the time talking to her to keep her relaxed. Perversely, Ouija Board the great international traveller, the horse so well attuned mentally that she can travel

Poetry in motion: Olivier Peslier takes Ouija Board to post before the Prince of Wales's Stakes.

between continents without turning a hair, can become very worked up in a horsebox. Chris Hinson does not mince his words about the more mundane part of Ouija Board's journeys – 'She can be an absolute bitch in a horsebox' – and recalls on the trip to Japan in 2005 she took out her agitation on the arm of the Japanese groom holding her 'until it was black and blue.'

On arrival at Ascot, Pat settled Ouija Board in her box at the racecourse stables and left her in peace, returning early in the afternoon to start getting her ready for the race: 'That day something told me she was going to win. There was always a very intelligent air about her, but at Ascot she felt extra-special. In the pre-parade she started pulling me round, which she never normally did, and Robin agreed that she had never felt so good or so strong. Her skin seemed to have taken on an extra sheen, almost transparent. She wasn't sweating – though it was a hot day – but she was clearly gearing herself up to run for her life. She was in her element.'

If Ouija Board was ready to run for her life, she needed to be, for the opposition was red-hot. With Frankie claimed by Godolphin to ride Electrocutionist and Kieren riding Ace for Coolmore, Ed had booked the top French jockey Olivier Peslier, and the competition was fierce. Electrocutionist, who, ridden by Frankie, had won the Dubai World Cup that (for us) dismal evening back in March, was favourite, rivalled in the betting by another hugely impressive winner that day at Nad Al

The Prince of Wales's Stakes: a hugely deserved pat for Ouija Board from Olivier Peslier as she beats Electrocutionist (Frankie Dettori) ... and (right) Pat Evens, grinning through the pain of a cracked rib, leads her back in.

Sheba, David Junior. Neither horse had run since then, and as both were very clearly at the top of their form while Ouija Board had not won since Hong Kong in December, it was not surprising that we were not expected to beat them, and Ouija Board started at the retrospectively giveaway price of 8-1.

Peslier rode a peach of a race. On the long pull up from Swinley Bottom he had Ouija Board settled in fifth place, travelling beautifully and all looking well under control, and then early in the straight came the most glorious sight: her jockey looking to the right and to the left, sublimely content in the knowledge that his horse was

Receiving the trophy from The Prince of Wales – with The Duke of Devonshire, Her Majesty's Representative at Ascot, on the left.

travelling best of all and that when he asked her to go, she would go. He did not go for what seemed a long time, and when he finally pressed the button she surged past all the others with an imperious turn of foot. Up in the Royal Box, decorum went out the window and the noise level shot off the scale as the whole place erupted in a clamour which did not subside until Ouija Board had pulled up and was returning toward us. Her winning margin over Electrocutionist was only half a length, but her superiority over the top colts was there for all to see.

Leading Ouija Board in after she had won a Group 1 race at Royal Ascot – and won in such magnificent style – was for me undoubtedly one of the highlights of her whole career. As during the final stages of the Oaks, I felt like I was walking on air. Less fortunate as we returned to the winner's enclosure was Pat Evens, who had been watching the race from near the winning post with Robin Trevor-Jones: 'I was shaking like a jelly during the race, but when Ouija Board went past the winning post Robin threw his arms around me and hoisted me into the air. As I came down to earth I heard a sharp snap, and realised that I had cracked a rib.' Pat bravely omitted to mention this as she led Ouija Board back past a delirious crowd.

After receiving the trophy from The Prince of Wales we took it back to the Royal Box, where it was enthroned on the table as we ate tea, and later that evening it sat on the dinner table at Bagshot, placed there at about the same time as the mare herself, who, according to Pat Evens, 'always knew when she was nearly home', started administering a succession of hefty kicks to the wall of the horsebox as it approached Newmarket.

The Royal Ascot victory was indisputably one of Ouija Board's greatest moments, and it was not lost on me that she had won despite our having to discard the superstition of wearing our usual race-day outfits. While I disapproved of breaking superstition, as she had won I said on air to Clare Balding, who was presenting the meeting for BBC television, that I would now have to pay for both Cazzy and Becky's outfits!

With Ouija Board back in the winning groove we set our sights on the next ten-furlong highlight of the summer, the Coral-Eclipse Stakes at Sandown Park two and a half weeks later, traditionally the first big middle-distance race of the year when the top three-year-olds take on the older horses. But in 2006 only two of the nine runners were three-year-olds – Aidan O'Brien-trained Aussie Rules, who had won the French equivalent of the Two Thousand Guineas, the Poule d'Essai des Poulains, and Snoqualmie Boy, who had finished unplaced behind Sir Percy in the Derby and had then won the Hampton Court Stakes at Royal Ascot. Two of the horses whom Ouija Board had beaten in the Prince of Wales's

Stakes, David Junior and Notnowcato, reopposed her, but since there was no obvious reason why they should reverse the placings now, her starting a warm favourite was only what we expected.

Sadly, though, Pat Evens was not at Sandown to lead her up. She had been forced to take time off to let the cracked rib recover, and later caught pneumonia and had to retire from working at Gainsborough Stables, though as often as possible she would return to see her heroine, laden with Ouija Board's favourite strong mints. Pat had played a significant role in Ouija Board's life, but now had to hand over the mantle of responsibility for the most popular horse in training to another of Ed's most experienced grooms, Vicki Clarke, and it was Vicki who had charge of the mare at Sandown.

At the start of Eclipse week we had been hoping that Olivier Peslier, who had ridden Ouija Board so exquisitely at Ascot, would be able to ride her again, but then we heard that his retainer to the Wertheimer family in France meant that his presence would be required elsewhere. Neither Frankie nor Kieren was available and Jamie Spencer was committed to David Junior, so we had to look further afield, and were happy to be able to secure the services of the Belgian-born and French-based riding phenomenon Christophe Soumillon, who in a short career had already won countless big races including the Prix de l'Arc de Triomphe on Dalakhani – though he sometimes seemed to attract more headlines with his celebratory gestures passing the winning post than through the quality of his riding.

I said earlier that a big race requires a big-race jockey, and Christophe Soumillon was

The Coral-Eclipse Stakes: David Junior (Jamie Spencer, quartered cap) wins from Notnowcato (Michael Kinane, yellow cap), with Ouija Board and Christophe Soumillon well behind.

certainly that, so Ed went ahead and booked him – thanks to the Aga Khan releasing him for Eclipse day from his contract to ride his horses, as he was such a fan of our mare – and the *Racing Post* marked the engagement of the eighth jockey to ride Ouija Board in her career with the headline, 'COME IN NUMBER 8!' As a guest on Channel Four Racing's *The Morning Line* on Eclipse day – Ouija Board's fame was now such that her owner could enjoy such an honour – I expressed myself happy with our choice of jockey,

but I was aware that Soumillon had one drawback: he was not particularly experienced at Sandown Park, which despite its sweeping home turn and long straight is considered by many jockeys a difficult course to get right if you are not familiar with it. The Analysis section of the *Racing Post* the following day encapsulated the sorry story:

Having held Ouija Board up near the back of the field, Soumillon found himself repeatedly boxed in from 2 furlongs out, with horses in front of him and Aussie Rules legitimately holding him in on the outside. When an opening came it soon closed again, and at one point approaching the furlong marker she stumbled slightly, though it made no difference as the damage was already done by that stage. Nobody can say for sure where she might have finished had Soumillon elected to produce her towards the outside, but when Ouija Board found herself on David Junior's inside in a tactical race at Royal Ascot she was able to drop back a shade and come round him, then quicken up so well that she beat him by 2 lengths. This time she never had the opportunity to unleash her trademark turn of foot.

With Ouija Board having such an unhappy time of it, eventually finishing only fifth, David Junior had been able to take advantage of her difficulties and run out an easy winner from Notnowcato. Thus the first two in the Eclipse had finished behind us at Royal Ascot, and, as we underwent a quick post-mortem with Soumillon under the Sandown Park trees, we knew that she had simply not had a fair crack of the whip.

Christophe Soumillon was widely castigated for the ride – the *Racing Post* paragraph above is moderate in its language, compared with some of the brickbats he received, and *Raceform* called it 'X-rated stuff' – and for how he seemed to find every blockage possible. It was clear from Ouija Board's previous races that she possessed a wonderful turn of foot, and the way to ride her was to pull wide and, when the time comes for her to go, press the button. As soon as Soumillon got off her he apologised to us, but I was rather annoyed when later I read that he had been absolving himself by stating in an interview with *Owner and Breeder* magazine that the mare

hadn't been herself, which we knew – and he knew – was not true.

So two of Ouija Board's last five races, the Sheema Classic and the Eclipse, had ended in a highly unsatisfactory manner, but it was always our way to shrug off the disappointments as rapidly as we could and move on to the next challenge, and since she remained so fresh and so well in herself, despite having sustained several cuts to her legs during her nightmare passage at Sandown Park, plans to give her a rest remained shelved – which is just as well, as her next race was to produce not only one of the peaks of her career, but one of the truly great moments of recent racing history.

The Nassau Stakes at Goodwood, over 1¼ miles for fillies and mares, has a long and highly distinguished history, though it had enjoyed Group 1 status only since 1999. The race was first run in 1840, and the list of its winners includes such famous names as Sceptre and Pretty Polly, two Turf immortals from the first decade of the twentieth century, Selene – dam of my great-grandfather's great horse Hyperion – in 1922, and more recently Aunt Edith, Roussalka, Ruby Tiger, Islington, Russian Rhythm and Alexander Goldrun (who had won in 2005 and was attempting a repeat in 2006). Ed had won the 2001 running with Sheikh Maktoum's Irish Oaks winner Lailani.

To add Ouija Board's name to such a roll of honour would be another major feather in her cap, but with an exceptionally strong field – *Raceform* was to call it 'one of the best ever fields lined up for this race' – we were very hopeful rather than confident as on the Saturday of the

Festival meeting in the first week of August, we made our way to Goodwood from Gatwick airport, to which British Airways had a convenient flight from where we had been on a family holiday in Majorca, from where heavy rain had delayed our return journey. Myself, Cazzy and Edward went to the races, while our nanny Carole took Hetty and Oliver – whose presence at the Yorkshire Oaks, in Dubai and at the Eclipse might have hinted at a jinx! – stayed with the Easyjet flight to Liverpool and thence to Knowsley.

As we drove down from Gatwick to Goodwood we learned about the drama on the M25 motorway the previous evening. I mentioned earlier how Ouija Board could become very stirred up in a horsebox, and sharing the frustration of every other Friday traveller on the M25 she had got herself so worked up that she managed to get one of her forelegs over the partition. As soon as Vicki Clarke realised what was happening, the box was steered onto the hard shoulder and Ouija Board extricated from her impossible position. She had suffered cuts on three legs but luckily was not too distressed by the incident and they were soon able to be on their way again. But the episode does illustrate how with racehorses, even the most mundane operation such as getting to the course can be fraught with hazards.

After the horrors of her journey, it was a relief to see Ouija Board looking so well in the parade ring, where the quality of the opposition indicated the scale of the task ahead of her: between them, the seven runners in the Nassau Stakes had won thirteen Group 1 races.

With Frankie back in the saddle, Ouija Board was a firm favourite. Second in the betting came Nannina, who had won the Coronation Stakes at Royal Ascot before finishing runner-up in the Falmouth Stakes at the Newmarket July Meeting, with the exceptionally tough Alexander Goldrun – like Ouija Board a five-year-old who seemed to get better with age – rivalling Nannina for second favouritism.

Alexander Goldrun was a remarkable mare. Trained in Ireland by Jim Bolger, she had really come to prominence when winning the Prix de l'Opera and then the Hong Kong Cup at Sha Tin as a three-year-old in 2004, and as a four-year-old had added to her Group 1 tally with

A memorable day at Goodwood made even more memorable for our elder son Edward by meeting his hero Johnny English – the actor Rowan Atkinson.

wins in the Pretty Polly Stakes at The Curragh and the Nassau Stakes. She was as tough as old boots, and a very hard horse to pass – as Ouija Board would soon be finding out – and came to Goodwood fresh from a repeat win in the Pretty Polly Stakes. Like Ouija Board at that stage, she had won five Group 1 races. (For the record, the other three Group 1 races won by the Nassau runners were the Coronation Stakes and 2005 Fillies' Mile won by Nannina, and the 2005 Moyglare Stud Stakes won by Chelsea Rose, who along with Nasheej, Echelon and Race For

Ouija Board (Frankie Dettori) and Alexander Goldrun (Kevin Manning) lock horns, before fighting out an unforgettable finish.

The Stars made up the Goodwood field.)

Because of the thunderstorms in Majorca which had delayed our flight to England we were late arriving for lunch with Janet and Charles March in The Duke of Richmond's box, where other guests included Lester Piggott and – much to Edward's delight and excitement – Rowan Atkinson: Edward was delighted to have his photograph taken with Johnny English! Charles and Janet, Earl and Countess of March, son and daughter-in-law of the Duke, were very welcoming to Edward, and their son Charles Settrington looked after him while we were away from the box as for very obvious health-and-

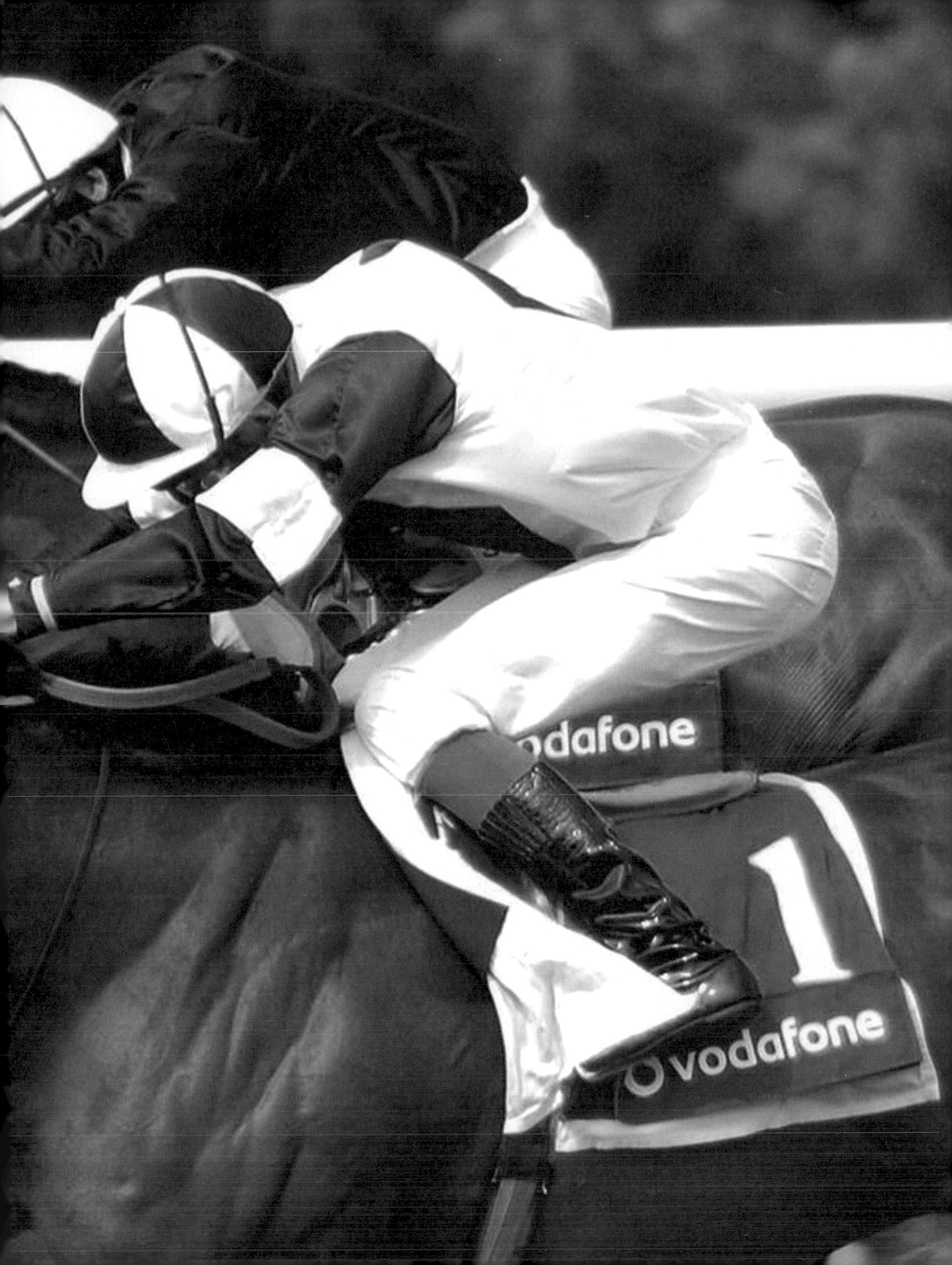
vodafone
1
vodafone

safety reasons under-twelves are not allowed in the paddock.

What was to become a famous race began in orthodox enough manner. Chelsea Rose made the early running at the sort of sedate pace which would not suit a horse with Ouija Board's stamina, and with fully three furlongs to go Frankie took up the running. Meanwhile Alexander Goldrun, who had been held up at the back of the field, started to make a forward move under Kevin Manning. With more than a furlong to run Ouija Board was still leading, but then Alexander Goldrun came up to join issue on the stands side and the pair started to pull clear of the others. A furlong out Alexander Goldrun's nose was in front and she looked like going on to a narrow victory, but Ouija Board simply would not be denied. Fighting back like a tigress, she started to rally, and with the crowd becoming increasingly hysterical, the two fought hammer and tongs, eyeball to eyeball, throughout the final furlong. Within a couple of strides of the winning post Ouija Board found slightly more, and just got her nose in front to win by a short head – or, as some more dramatically put it, a flared nostril. A titanic battle, and a close, but conclusive, verdict to us.

Sarah Aspinall's painting of the Nassau finish.

At least that's how I, watching the race from the Duke's box, saw it, and I hurried out of the box and down the stairs with Edward to the winner's enclosure, as I wanted to be sure of being on the spot to greet her when she returned. I was convinced that we'd won, and as I went down the steps to the winner's enclosure I heard the tannoy announce, 'The result of the photograph … First, number 4' – which was a relief but not a surprise as, from my view of the race, I was not expecting a photofinish to be called. In hindsight I realised that the view from the Duke's box, just after the finish, favours a horse on the far side.

As we waited in the unsaddling area for Ouija Board to return, it soon became clear that something strange was happening – because nothing was happening. Ouija Board and Frankie had not appeared. Where were they?

While we waited I watched, on the large screen beside the paddock, replay after replay of the race, and witnessed Ed's reaction, dropping his head onto the paddock rail every time he saw her cross the line. While I was confident that Ouija Board had won, Ed, who had watched the race on the paddock screen, was far from convinced.

After what seemed a very long time I sensed

a wave of excited applause coming up the walkway which leads into the Goodwood parade ring, off which the unsaddling enclosure is situated, and into view came ... not our mare, but the wonderfully brave Alexander Goldrun. That the beaten mare was greeted with a surge of appreciative and affectionate applause was a mark of what makes such an occasion on an English racecourse so very special. Whether racegoers had backed her or not was completely forgotten in the urge to salute a mare who had, in the words of *Raceform*, 'played a magnificent part in one of the greatest races ever seen at Goodwood – or anywhere else for that matter.' In truth, I found the reception for Alexander Goldrun as moving as that for Ouija Board shortly afterwards.

The official photofinish print.

But still she had not appeared. Where was she? I soon found out that Frankie, judging perfectly the mood of the crowd, who were in raptures over what they had just seen and were aware – though nothing had been finally decided – that she might not be seen on a British racecourse again, had taken Ouija Board on an unscheduled parade past the packed stands so that the whole crowd could show their appreciation.

But the formalities had to be gone through, and the applause continued as she proceeded up the walkway and into the unsaddling enclosure, where Frankie put the icing on the cake of the occasion with a spectacular flying dismount. 'Three cheers for Ouija Board!', someone in the crowd shouted, and the whole of Goodwood bellowed their appreciation.

I have never – before or since – seen Frankie so emotional. It has long been evident that he wears his heart on his sleeve in a manner unusual among Flat jockeys, but after the Nassau he was in seventh heaven, evidence of his genuine attachment to the mare. After the trophy presentation he shouted his usual nickname for me: 'Lordy! Have you seen the photo?' I hadn't, so he took me into the weighing room, where I saw for the first time just how close the race had been.

The fall-out from the Nassau Stakes was huge, and after such a race no excuse is needed for getting immersed in the feeling of well-being it generated, at Goodwood and way beyond. This is Lee Mottershead's report in the *Racing Post*:

A horserace, a special, wonderful horserace, can occasionally engender a sense of collective joy among those lucky enough to witness it in person. Those fortunate people present at

Goodwood yesterday know what such joy feels like. They were present for one of the finest contests ever staged on these rolling Sussex downs, a contest that crescendoed into a duel now forever etched in this place's history.

Ouija Board and Alexander Goldrun went into the Vodafone Nassau Stakes as heroines already. One a queen of England, one a darling of Ireland, they came together as five-year-olds each in possession of five Group 1 victories. Now one of them has six, after Ouija Board prevailed by the shortest of short heads, having slugged it out with her rival for more than a quarter-mile of undiluted pleasure.

Sent to the front early in the straight by Frankie Dettori, Ouija Board was joined by the defending Nassau champion soon after. The Irish invader then inched her nose in front, and probably kept it there until the final stride. But, in that stride, after a duel of epic proportions, it was the gallant Ouija Board whose nostrils were in front.

'It was pretty awesome,' said Ouija Board's owner Lord Derby, and it was. It was awesome enough for Dettori to parade his mount back in front of the stands, and awesome enough for the mare to receive the sort of rapturous reception that Goodwood has tended to reserve for the likes of Double Trigger and Persian Punch. 'Three cheers for Ouija Board,' ordered one racegoer around the winner's enclosure. Three cheers were enthusiastically given.

'I hope everyone enjoyed it – it sounded like they did,' said Ouija Board's trainer Ed Dunlop, who on Wednesday landed the meeting's other Group 1 race, the Sussex Stakes, with Court Masterpiece.

'It was an amazing race to watch and we

Racing at its breathless best as brilliant Ouija Board (top) battles bac to thwart Alexander Goldrun in the Nassau Stakes at Goodwood

were lucky enough to win it,' he added. 'It was a great testament to both horses, a great race, and I'm delighted we've won. It's been a great week. We've won the two Group 1s at Goodwood, and it doesn't get much better than that.'

Having conceded that 'we've had plans all year and broken them,' Dunlop could reveal no certain targets for Ouija Board, although the Breeders' Cup appears to remain the main objective.

However, while Ouija Board seems sure to head to the paddocks next year, for Alexander Goldrun that may not be so.

'She could be around for another year,' said Bolger, delighted with his own stable star. 'I've never heard such applause for a runner-up – what a great race! I've never been less put out after being beaten a short head. We'd been intending to run in the Irish Champion Stakes, and nothing that's happened here need change that.'

Equally content was John Gosden, whose Nannina took an honourable third, two lengths adrift of the big two. 'We're really thrilled with her run,' he said. 'She was only ever going to be third, but we were really pleased with the way she was running on at the finish.'

Yet, with all due respect to Nannina, this was a two-horse race, but a two-horse race won by the horse the crowd wanted to see win. On this most English of soil, they applauded Ouija Board on the way to the start, roared her home, then cheered her back. 'She's one of the all-time favourite horses of England,' said a jubilant Dettori, summing things up to perfection. 'A special filly, one of a kind.'

Peter Thomas in the same paper struck a similar note:

There are some days in life you know you'll treasure until the time comes to start pushing up daisies, some sporting moments you'll hold dear until your powers of recall disappear into the ether, and if you were at Goodwood yesterday and don't know what I mean, you should probably check yourself in to the local infirmary and ask them to look for vital signs.

The Vodafone Nassau Stakes was, quite simply, one of the greatest clashes of Titans since, well, since the Titanic hit the iceberg, on a par with that memorable afternoon when the Irresistible Force met the Immovable Object at level weights and fought out an unforgettable dead-heat.

And, luckily for all concerned, this hammer-and-tongs battle was conducted in front of a crowd that, unlike its counterparts at some other summer festivals, combined knowledgeable appreciation with naive enthusiasm in equal and copious measure.

Irish maestro Jim Bolger was not alone in being stunned by the level of applause that greeted the bold runner-up Alexander Goldrun as she dipped into the reserve tank of her energy to return to the enclosure. But for all her contribution to the excitement, the moment belonged to the horse that the British racing public has taken to its heart like no other.

For all the right reasons (sporting owner, proper-bloke trainer, fearless campaign manager, iron constitution, etc., etc.), Ouija Board has been winched on to the pedestal reserved exclusively *for those who reach beyond the constraints of mere sporting achievement to earn the less bankable but infinitely more rewarding prize of our love and respect. Yesterday was the day when these elusive concepts were distilled and trapped in a bottle labelled 'Essence of Racehorse'.*

Remarkably for a beast that has always struck this observer as being one of the least complicated beings ever to tread the turf, Ouija Board has found her path to glory blocked by all manner of obstacles, not least of them jockey error and rank ill-fortune.

But yesterday, with Frankie Dettori returning to the saddle that has played host in recent times to more small people than Snow White's cottage, there were no mistakes.

Operating at a trip that figures at the low end of her stamina range, she was wisely used to the full by Dettori, taking up the running early enough to avoid an undignified late sprint, steadily enough to conserve the vigour required to claw back the neck advantage Alexander Goldrun wrested from her at the start of their unflinching duel.

'She's one of my all-time favourite fillies, one of Britain's favourites,' said Dettori, 'and thankfully, I didn't mess up.'

Given the chance to be the best, Ouija Board rarely comes off second best. Six times a Group 1 winner now, she may yet have more delights to share with us, and if they must be doled out on foreign shores, they will be worth travelling for. There have certainly been worse 12-1 shots for the Arc than this handsome mare.

In light of the fact that Lord Derby has been to the well with his pride and joy more times than we could ever have hoped for (so often, in fact, that her doubters have long been expecting her relentless campaign to take its toll), it may seem churlish to complain that he may soon take her from us in a bid to produce lots more little Ouija Boards. Of course, she's got to go some time, but she'll leave a great big hole in the Turf when she does.

And this is an editorial in *The Sportsman*:

Those of us with long memories still bore the younger generations about the epic battle between Grundy and Bustino in the King George of 1975, arguing it was the 'greatest' race.

When Hurricane Run won the Ascot showpiece last week, many who saw it believed it was the race of the decade.

Thanks to Ouija Board and Alexander Goldrun, yesterday's nail-biting Nassau Stakes at Glorious Goodwood spectacularly put paid to those claims.

These two superstar mares went head to head up the long Goodwood straight with neither giving an inch. Alexander Goldrun hit the front two out and with a furlong to run had neck to spare, looking as if she was going to land a sixth Group 1 – but Frankie Dettori and Ouija Board had other ideas.

As they crossed the line Lord Derby's Classic-winning mare snatched the verdict by the width of a cigarette paper.

The Irish raider will always be remembered as the one who came second in this great tussle, but that will not concern trainer Jim Bolger, who was quite rightly proud of his stable star's performance.

So popular was Ouija Board's brave victory that as she returned to the paddock the crowd erupted with three cheers. These scenes – normally reserved for Cheltenham in March – are not generally witnessed on the more sedate Sussex Downs in August.

If ever there was a case for keeping horses in training after their three-year-old days are over, this was the finest example because between them the two mares have bagged an incredible eleven Group 1 wins – it's 6-5 Ouija Board.

Sadly, this was almost certainly the last time either mare will race in Britain, but there is little chance either will be forgotten.

At a time when racing has been attracting all the wrong headlines [on account of allegations of race-fixing, etc.], these two courageous mares put racing back in the spotlight for all the right reasons.

I mentioned that *Sportsman* editorial a few days later in an email to Alexander Goldrun's trainer Jim Bolger:

What a race. We are both so lucky to be involved with such wonderful mares. Saturday was one of those races that will be remembered by everyone for a long time to come. I see the Sportsman *in its leader yesterday compared it to the epic Bustino/Grundy battle in the King George.*

It truly was Glorious Goodwood on Saturday. I felt so sorry that there had to be a first and second place after such a battle. Maybe progress is not always good – without the technology we would have had a very fair dead heat. Alexander Goldrun got such a cheer and applause as she came into the winner's enclosure. That for a second was as unprecedented as three cheers was for Ouija Board. Can there be a better case for keeping a filly/mare in training for a extra season or two?

I have never felt more for the connections in a horse defeated by one of mine. Thank you for your kind words saying you were not as upset as usual to be behind by a nostril on the line.

We may meet again and who knows what the outcome will be? The racing public will be salivating at the thought.

Jim Bolger replied:

Many thanks for your email. You must have more energy than Ouija Board. I would have thought you would need another forty-eight hours to get around to communicating with the vanquished.

It was a very kind act on your part and a first for me in almost thirty years of training racehorses – you scored a double at the weekend – well done.

I never felt any sorrow for Dick Hern or Joe Mercer all those years ago and now I am not entitled to any self pity as I fully appreciate what a privilege it is to be in a position to put you, Ed, Frankie and Ouija Board under such pressure, especially on a day where everything went smoothly for all competitors.

I wish you every success in your future racing endeavours and hope you do the big one at Epsom – only please don't make us all look bad by doing it with just one in training!

The Irish Champion Stakes: Ouija Board and Jamie Spencer come to tackle Dylan Thomas and Kieren Fallon – but just miss out after a stirring struggle.

When the dust from that epic and unforgettable occasion died down, it started to sink in that the Nassau had been Ouija Board's last race in England. Or had it? Ed was keen on an autumn campaign of Breeders' Cup and the Far East, and Cazzy, Peter and I all supported this fully. But we would need to get another race into her before the Breeders' Cup – held in 2006 at Churchill Downs, Louisville, home of the Kentucky Derby – as that trip involved huge expense (not least the entry fee, which had increased since the 2005 running to $120,000 for us – though it should be pointed out that the prize money had also been increased) and we would have to be sure that Ouija Board was on song. The Champion Stakes at Newmarket in mid-October was a possibility, while other European options were the Irish Champion Stakes at Leopardstown in mid-September and the Arc or Prix de l'Opera at Longchamp on the first Sunday of October. But the Champion Stakes was uncomfortably close to the Breeders' Cup, and there was a likelihood of unsuitably soft ground at both Newmarket and Longchamp.

Whichever way we looked at it, the Irish Champion Stakes was the best option, so we trained our sights firmly on Leopardstown on 9 September. Naturally we were anxious to avoid giving Ouija Board too hard a race, and daily during the week leading up to the Saturday I bombarded poor Tom Burke, manager at Leopardstown, with anxious enquiries about the state of the ground. In the event we had nothing to worry about on that score as the official going was good to firm, and looked set fair as we sat down to lunch with Niall Quirk, dressage trainer of the Irish team, and our friends David and Elizabeth Steer, who live near Knowsley and have been very influential in developing Cazzy's passion for dressage.

Ouija Board faced only four opponents, but one of these was none other than Alexander Goldrun. Another was Aidan O'Brien-trained Dylan Thomas, who after being beaten by a short head and a head when third in the Derby had won the Irish Derby in good style, and then disappointed behind Notnowcato in the International Stakes at York. Ouija Board had beaten Notnowcato at Royal Ascot (though the form had been reversed in the Eclipse), so should have had every prospect of beating Dylan Thomas, and the prospect of a return match with Alexander Goldrun was one to set the pulse racing. With Kieren Fallon committed to Dylan Thomas for Coolmore and Frankie at York to ride Sixties Icon in the relocated St Leger – which he won – we were again having to find a jockey for Ouija Board, and were able to secure the services of Jamie Spencer, who had ridden her twice as a two-year-old and then in the unfortunate outing in the Prince of Wales's Stakes at York.

The Irish betting public were minded to forgive Dylan Thomas his lapse at York and sent him off 13-8 favourite, with Ouija Board on 11-4 and Alexander Goldrun 3-1; the other two runners were Mustameet (8-1), trained by Kevin Prendergast, and Aidan O'Brien's second string Ace (12-1).

Ace made the early running, with Ouija Board settled in third, and was still leading when they entered the straight, where Dylan Thomas took up the running. Then Jamie decided it was time to make his move and, with a furlong and half still to go, sent Ouija Board into the lead as he saw when he looked over his right shoulder that Alexander Goldrun was starting to make her move. But for once Jim Bolger's mare failed to show her best form, and with Dylan Thomas apparently disposed of, it looked as if Ouija Board was going to score a narrow victory. Then inside the final furlong Kieren conjured a fresh run out of Dylan Thomas, who started to rally, and although Ouija Board tried her level best to hang on, he had roused Dylan Thomas to such a pitch that close home he got his head in front again, and won by a neck. No wonder they call Kieren 'The Assassin'.

It is never satisfactory to be beaten by a horse that you've already gone past, and Jamie came in for some criticism that he had made his move too soon. That at least was the conclusion of the *Raceform* experts, and the fact that the same publication declared Ouija Board's performance a lifetime best judged on the Racing Post Ratings figure she had returned, that was scant consolation for a narrow defeat. (Whether ratings are to Ouija Board's credit or to her detriment, I have tried not to get too worked up about them. She is a racehorse, and for me it is how she races that matters, whatever the rating she is deemed to have registered.)

Disappointing but far from disheartening was the verdict on our Leopardstown trip, and we started to discuss whether she should attempt the Arc. Ed was keen to have a go, but I remained convinced that the ground would be too soft for her. As it turned out the ground in Paris dried out, and the 2006 Arc was run on

ground officially described as good, so in retrospect I was wrong not to have let her take her chance.

In any case, it was now full speed ahead to Churchill Downs, where the Filly and Mare Turf would again be the target.

Ouija Board flew to Kentucky without turning a hair, but again her regular companion Chris Hinson was not able to be with her: sadly a bout of meningitis had landed him in hospital for a week, and his role of Ouija Board's exercise rider was again taken by Jason Tate.

Yet again – for the third year running – the build-up to the race was dominated by the wet weather and its likely effect on the going. Picking up a *Racing Post* on the way to catch our flight at Heathrow, the first headline I saw read: 'DUNLOP VOICES FEARS OVER SLOW GROUND FOR OUIJA BID' – a headline almost identical to the one at the equivalent time two years earlier, and even to the one the previous year. I took this as a good omen.

After a four-hour wait to change planes at Chicago, where Cazzy, Kath Goff (wife of bloodstock agent Tom) and I had a revolting fast-food dinner, we arrived in Louisville late on the Thursday night, tired but keen to meet up with the Dunlops (who had been there two days) and Stanleys (who had arrived an hour earlier). We were staying in the Brown Hotel ('Official Breeders' Cup VIP Headquarters'), and once we'd got to our room I decided that the top two priorities were stashing our passports away in the safe which big hotels customarily provide, and going down to the bar to meet up for a drink. The trouble was, I could not locate the safe in our room. I phoned down to reception.

'I'm sorry, but I can't find the safe in my room.'

'That, sir, is because there is no safe in your room.'

'Isn't that a bit unusual for a big hotel?'

'Not in Louisville, it's not.'

But Caroline the concierge could not have tried harder to make our stay in Louisville (which not even the locals claim to be one of the most vibrant cities in the world, though the Muhammad Ali Museum celebrates the city's most illustrious son in appropriate fashion) as comfortable and enjoyable as possible, and book whatever we needed, such as finding a hairdresser able to make appointments at short notice on a Saturday. I was particularly struck by the prints which adorned our hotel bedroom: over each bed was a reproduction of the painting *The Earl of Derby's Staghounds* by Sartorius!

The next morning we were up early to head down to the track at 6.30 a.m., accompanied by Peter and Frances and by my mother and stepfather, who had flown in the night before. It was very exciting to see the twin spires on the historic Churchill Downs grandstand, but we had been greeted by a cold morning with heavy frost – so heavy that the opening of the turf track, on which Ouija Board was to canter, was delayed, and at one point there was a serious possibility that it would not be opened that day at all, an injection of drama which we could have done without. Luckily it was decided that track work could go ahead, and she managed to complete her preparation without a hiccup.

Whatever happened in the Breeders' Cup and

the expected Far East trip which would follow it, we knew that Ouija Board's illustrious racing career was fast approaching its conclusion, and we had long been mulling over the best way for her to start her new life as a broodmare in 2007. Given her own achievements it was vital that she be sent to stallions of the highest order and many of these are standing in the USA. If she was to visit an American stallion, it would be easiest for her to do so as a maiden broodmare as, all being well, in subsequent years she would be in foal at the appropriate time, and would therefore have to deliver the foal in the USA before being

Trackwork: Frankie tucked up against the Kentucky cold.

covered by that season's chosen sire, and practical difficulties, while not insurmountable, would add to the logistical problems of sending her so far.

For such reasons our inclination was strongly in favour of having her covered by a US stallion in 2007, and although we had yet to reach a final decision, one possibility whom we were considering very seriously was Kingmambo, a son of the brilliant Miesque (who had won back-to-back runnings of the Breeders' Cup Mile in 1987 and 1988) who had himself been a top-notch miler, winning the Poule d'Essai des Poulains (French equivalent of the Two Thousand Guineas), St James's Palace Stakes and Prix du Moulin in 1993).

He was now sixteen years old but still a highly successful stallion, and the speed which he had shown to win such races was an attractive element to blend with Ouija Board's stamina.

So on the Friday morning we took the opportunity to visit Will Farish and his staff at Lane's End Farm, where Kingmambo stood. Kingmambo is visited by sixty-odd mares a year and, not surprisingly for a stallion of his reputation, does not cover maiden mares. But we were assured that, in the light of Ouija Board's

status and of the personal connection through Peter, who had worked with the Farishes in the 1980s, an exception would be made in her case.

My rather poor snapshot of Kingmambo on the day we met Ouija Board's prospective mate at Lane's End Farm.

At Lane's End we also met Will's son Bill Farish (now Chairman of Breeders' Cup), Simon Marsh (who manages the Watership Down Stud for Lord and Lady Lloyd-Webber) and Will Sporborg (son of Christopher Sporborg, a prominent Jockey Club member), who has been confined to a wheelchair following a riding accident, and we were all taken on a great tour of the enormous – by English standards – stud, which covers some 3,000 acres. It was very good to get Peter's input into our discussions at Lane's End, as the moment was getting ever closer when he would be taking over management of Ouija Board from Ed, who had been in charge of her day-to-day existence for four years. (While we were watching Kingmambo walk up, Peter pointed out to our mother that twenty years ago he had been raking the gravel at this magnificent stud!)

The following morning, the day of the Breeders' Cup, I started my usual pre-race routine with a run along the banks of the River Ohio, the massive waterway which cuts through Louisville. I find running an effective way of clearing the head, steadying the nerves, and giving me a hour of peace to calm my nerves before being thrust into the bustle of the racetrack. It was wonderful to be in the home of the Kentucky Derby, and I undertook any number of interviews about the relationship between the name Derby and the race – and in particular the pronunciation of Durrby as opposed to Darby.

We had rented a stretch limo – as you seem to in the USA, instead of the minibus in the UK – for our party of ten: myself and Cazzy, Ed and Becky, Peter and Frances, Bill and Rosie Spiegelberg, Tom and Kath Goff.

At the racetrack on Breeders' Cup day we had a lunch table in the US Jockey Club area, where on arrival we availed ourselves of Bloody Marys (which by now had become something of a superstition on the days of Ouija Board's races), then a bottle or two of Dom Perignon to raise the spirits.

Vicki Clarke, who looked after Ouija Board at Gainsborough Stables, does not ride her, but so devoted was she to her charge that she had asked to take a few days' holiday in order to go to Churchill Downs and lead up her beloved mare, and at the track we were again struck by how wide was Ouija Board's appeal, and how far the mare had risen in the esteem and affection of the American racing public. Everyone wanted to know how she was, and there was a real appreciation for her making the trip to the Breeder's Cup for the third time. In the run-up to the race the press was full of stories about her, and most of the local pundits predicted that she would win the Filly and Mare Turf. With Frankie again booked, all the omens looked positive.

I was not so confident, as no Breeders' Cup race can ever be easy, and her nine opponents included some very good fillies and mares. Film Maker, who had finished runner-up to Ouija Board in 2004 and third when she came second in 2005, was back for another crack, but second favourite to us, and strongly fancied locally, was the three-year-old Wait A While, considered the best turf filly in the USA. Satwa Queen, runner-up to Mandesha in the Prix de l'Opera at Longchamp on Arc day, and Germance were challengers from France.

But in truth the Filly and Mare Turf looked Ouija Board's for the taking, and when in the paddock beforehand Frankie declared that he was sure he would finish 'thereabouts', I reminded him of how cross he had been after they had finished 'thereabouts' in Hong Kong back in April.

The race itself needs little describing. Frankie

The 2006 Breeders' Cup Filly and Mare Turf: Ouija Board, Frankie, and the famous twin spires of Churchill Downs.

kept Ouija Board mid-division in the early part of the race, and going down the back straight gradually improved his position down the outside. Coming round the home turn they were in about fourth place, then approaching the final furlong started to take on the leaders, hitting the front inside the last 200 yards and staying on stoutly. I will never forget the racecourse commentator calling her home with the words, 'And here comes the scintillating superstar!'

Ed and Becky always watched Ouija Board's races separate from us at ground level, while we found a good place in the owners' viewing area, but whatever the vantage point, seeing Ouija Board coming round the home turn so full of running and then mounting her challenge on the outside left not a moment of doubt. She was always going to win, and when she crossed the line 2¼ lengths ahead of Film Maker – one place behind Ouija Board yet again! – there was an explosion of joy. We raced down to the dirt track along which she would return to the winner's circle, and to watch that huge American crowd clapping and cheering her to the echo as Frankie steered her back towards us brought a lump to my throat.

To have won two Breeders' Cup races – the only British-trained horse to have done so, and just the seventh in the event's history – and finished runner-up in another made her the most successful horse in the history of the event, but they were cheering more than that. They were cheering her durability and her inability to give other than her best, and of course they were cheering her sheer brilliance. The crowd did not move from the stand for a good while, keen to marvel at Ouija Board for as long as they could.

Frankie – who naturally graced the occasion with a flying dismount – was appropriately delighted, and was to become even happier when winning the Breeders' Cup Turf later in the afternoon on Red Rocks.

Each Breeders' Cup race is followed by a press conference, and, as there was an enormous crowd to be negotiated and as I was helping Will Sporborg manoeuvre his wheelchair, I was a little late arriving. As I entered the room, Ed was being asked whether Ouija Board was certainly retiring at the end of the year, which he was able to deflect with 'Here's the owner now: is this definitely Ouija Board's last season?' – a question he was very keen to hear answered in the negative, though he knew that Cazzy, Peter and I had made our minds up and would not be deflected. (John McCririck later demanded on television that Cazzy withdraw conjugal rights unless I agreed to keep the mare in training as a six-year-old, but even the threat of such drastic action would not deflect me!)

Then Frankie was asked whether Ouija Board was the best filly or mare he had ever ridden and, mindful as ever of his obligation to his major employer Godolphin, produced the highly tactful answer that she had to be right up there with the very best.

We returned to England, and almost straight into the awards season. In the last two months of the year the racing industry stages a succession of awards events, at several of which, thanks to Ouija Board, we have been fortunate enough to win in various categories.

First out of the awards stalls in 2006 was the Cartier evening in mid November. On the morning of the awards dinner I awoke with a raging temperature, and felt so ill in the evening that I could neither eat nor drink. But I did manage to muster the strength to collect, on behalf of Ouija Board, awards both for Older Horse of the Year and the top award of the evening, Horse of the Year. This was the second occasion she had won Horse of the Year – the first was in 2004 – the only horse in the history of the Cartier Awards, which were founded in 1991, to win that title twice. It was once again a great pleasure to collect the awards from our good friends Arnaud Bamberger and Harry Herbert.

Gary Middlebrook, a fellow director of Haydock Park racecourse, won the sprinter award with Reverence, winner of the Nunthorpe Stakes at York and the Sprint Cup at Haydock. So between us, two directors of Haydock won five Group 1 races and three Cartier Awards in 2006. (Not since the heyday of Robert Sangster had so many Group 1 races been won by the Haydock board.) And I was delighted that Jim Bolger, who took the narrow defeat of Alexander Goldrun at

Goodwood so graciously, won awards with both of his top-notch two-year-olds, Teofilo and Finsceal Beo. The award for Three-Year-Old Filly of the Year went to Mandesha, the Prix Vermeille winner owned by the Aga Khan's daughter Princess Zahra, and at the dinner she told me that she intended to race the filly as a four-year-old, as she had been so impressed and excited by what Ouija Board had achieved by being kept in training.

But no matter how many awards she was winning, Ouija Board still had races ahead of her, and as the Japan Cup was only three weeks after the Breeders' Cup she did not return to Newmarket, but was flown from Churchill Downs to Tokyo via New York. For her brief stopover in New York she was accommodated at Belmont Park, where on the morning of a non-racing day a crowd of forty people suddenly materialised trackside when word got round that Ouija Board was going to canter on the track. This mark of her international appeal was repeated in Tokyo, where at the quarantine unit at Cheroi people would gather just to see her appear on the training track.

The Japan Cup on 26 November, in which

Menu cover for the Japan Cup welcome party.

again Frankie would ride, would be Ouija Board's ninth race of the year – considerably more than she had contested annually before (three as a two-year-old, five at three, and five again at four) – and her ninth Group 1 of the year, and the way she had maintained her form at the highest level since Dubai way back in March, without ever getting the substantial break we had planned for her, was a mammoth tribute to the skills of Ed and his staff at Gainsborough Stables. Sheikh Maktoum al Maktoum, who owned the stables and was hugely influential in Ed's career, had sadly died in January, and Ed had announced that he would become a public trainer from the start of 2007. There could be no finer advertisement of his skills than the way he handled Ouija Board. She would not have been the horse she was without him: he handled her – and, it has to be said, he handled her owner – flawlessly.

As before, the trip to Japan was accompanied by hospitality of a high order, and as before Ouija Board ran a gallant race but was beaten.

There were only two overseas challengers for the 2006 Japan Cup, Ouija Board and, from the Chantilly stable of John Hammond (whose wife

Georgina is Becky Dunlop's step-sister), Freedonia, the filly who had finished fourth to Mandesha in the Prix Vermeille and then runner-up in the Turf Classic at Belmont Park in early October. One probable reason for the paucity of foreign raiders is that the home contingent was exceptionally strong, headed by the national hero Deep Impact and the first horse ever to defeat him, Heart's Cry; another is the challenge of keeping a European horse going so late in the season, and the fact that Ouija Board was turning up fit and well for her second consecutive Japan Cup is yet another feather in the cap of Ed and the Gainsborough Stable staff.

Deep Impact had a huge following in Japan, where he was regarded with a mixture of reverence and awe. From twelve career starts he had been beaten only twice: by Heart's Cry in the Arima Kinen in December 2005, and when running third in his only race outside Japan, the Prix de l'Arc de Triomphe at Longchamp in October. Here a huge contingent of fans backed him so heavily on the pari-mutuel that at one stage his odds were 1-10, and even his returned price of 1-2 was ludicrously unrealistic against the standard of competition he was facing, which included the previous year's winner Hurricane Run and the great French mare Pride. Deep Impact finished third behind Rail Link and Pride, but was subsequently disqualified when it was discovered – highly embarrassingly for Japanese racing – that his post-race sample

had shown traces of a prohibited substance. Now back on his home territory and in front of his adoring fans, he was widely considered unbeatable.

Heart's Cry, who since beating Deep Impact in the Arima Kinen had won the Sheema Classic in Dubai – with Ouija Board and Kieren Fallon that desperately disappointing fourth – had gone to England and run a marvellous race to come third, beaten only one length, behind Hurricane Run and Electrocutionist in the King George VI and Queen Elizabeth Diamond Stakes at Ascot. He looked to have a chance of beating Deep Impact again, starting at nearly 6-1 as opposed to Deep Impact's price of 30-100; Ouija Board was the third most heavily backed runner, going off at 152-10 on the local pari-mutuel.

We had talked tactics with Frankie, and our plan was a simple one: get behind Deep Impact and go when he goes, then hope to have the speed to get past him. But we were thwarted by the Deep Impact camp's own tactics, which were to hold him up in last and make a late run in the straight. You can't track a horse who is running last, so Frankie kept Ouija Board in second last, trying to anticipate when the favourite would make his move and then go with him. There was nothing wrong in the tactic, and Frankie duly made his move as soon as Deep Impact went past him on the outside. But although she stayed on gamely she could not get in a serious blow as

Ouija Board's last race: a fine third behind the mighty Deep Impact in the 2006 Japan Cup.

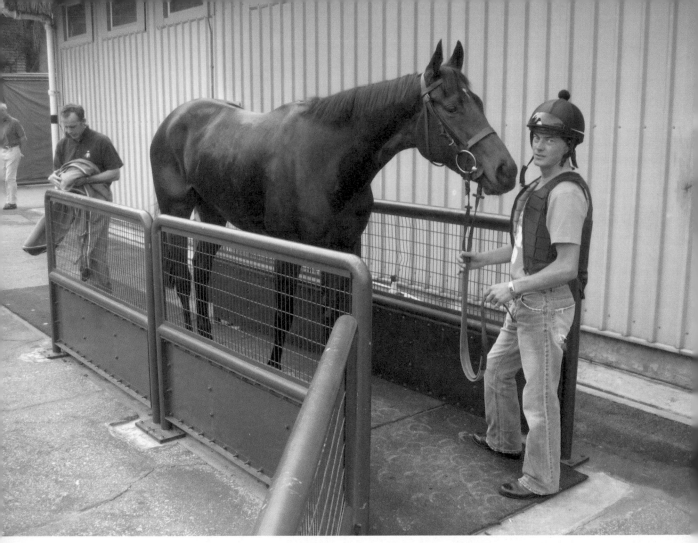

Yutaka Take on Deep Impact – at his best a truly magnificent racehorse – hammered up the straight to win by two lengths from Dream Passport, with Ouija Board half a length back in third. Heart's Cry was a highly disappointing tenth of the eleven runners.

As Frankie rode her down the tunnel towards the unsaddling enclosure, he told us how upset Ouija Board was that she had not won, and that she needed lots of pats to cheer her up!

Ouija Board had run yet another marvellous race, and in finishing third earned the equivalent of £310,912, almost as much as she had picked up by winning both the Prince of Wales's Stakes and Nassau Stakes.

This brought her career earnings up to £3,510,682 (of which only two thirds came from races she won, which just illustrates how much can be accrued from being placed in the big international races). If she finished first or second in the Hong Kong Vase two weeks later, she would pass the total earned by Sheikh Mohammed's great globe-trotter Singspiel and become the highest-earning British-trained horse in the history of racing. In addition, she would equal the record of the great Allez France of eight Group 1 races won by a filly or mare.

With those happy prospects on the horizon, we returned to London for ten days while Ouija Board flew straight from Tokyo to Hong Kong, where she arrived at Sha Tin on the Tuesday evening after the Fuchu race. As usual, her heroics had taken little out of her, and all looked set for her final hurrah.

Spare a thought here for Jason Tate and

Robin Trevor-Jones, who had been Ouija Board's companions since she left Newmarket for Churchill Downs in late October and would remain with her until the conclusion of her Hong Kong adventure. By the end of their stint they would have been away for some nine weeks, living above her box in Japan and in nearby hotels in Kentucky and Hong Kong and never off duty, exercising her every day and weighing her twice a day to monitor her wellbeing, in addition to the usual duties of a groom. Their devotion to 'Mother' cannot be exaggerated.

My diary for the week before the great Cathay Pacific

Ouija Board (with Jason Tate) and Alexander Goldrun (with Lee Smyth), joint heroines of the famous Nassau Stakes, meet again in Hong Kong.

Hong Kong International Races were to be held on Sunday 10 December was pretty crowded even without flying out to Hong Kong to see our heroine in her last race.

On the Monday I went to the Derby Awards lunch of the Horserace Writers' and Photographers' Association, of which I am patron. The lunch is sponsored by the bookmaker Blue Square, and each table was invited to enter a competition predicting the winners of the various awards. The tie-breaker question in the event of two or more tables registering the same score was, in due deference to the HWPA's patron: 'Multiply the number of furlongs Ouija Board has run over, by the number of jockeys who have ridden her, by the number of races in which she has run.' The answer (and no correspondence can be entered into) is 40,832 (arrived at by multiplying 232 furlongs by 8 jockeys by 22 races) – but in the event the tie-break was not needed.

Christmas was fast approaching, and on the Wednesday we were proud parents watching nine-year-old Henrietta singing in the choral group and French choir at her school, then four-year-old Oliver as narrator in his nativity play – after which we made our way to Heathrow for the flight to Hong Kong. Once again our wonderful nanny Carole Dowson had to look after the children 24/7 in the absence of their parents.

We arrived in Hong Kong on the Thursday afternoon and went straight to the racecourse to see Ouija Board: she had enjoyed a less than rigorous piece of work with Frankie on the turf track that morning, and looked in wonderful shape.

On the Friday morning we were at the track early to watch her final exercise on the all-weather track under Jason Tate. All seemed fine, and we were happily looking forward to the race on Sunday as we went off to the gala party at Stanley Harbour. We had an extra reason for celebration that day – or rather three extra reasons, as we had been told that at the Racehorse Owners' Association awards dinner the previous evening Ouija Board had won Older Horse of the Year and Horse of the Year, and I had again been named Owner of the Year. Anticipating such an outcome, when we knew we would be in the Far East on the evening of the dinner I asked Pat Cronin, who had brought Ouija Board into the world, and Chris Hinson, who had done so much to educate her, to represent us.

But the Hong Kong trip had a sting in the tail. Saturday began with our customary visit to the quarantine barn at Sha Tin to watch Ouija Board's final preparation, a few rounds of the trotting circuit under regular work-rider Jason Tate. She came back into the barn, and a few minutes later Ed Dunlop and I remained there while she was led out again to trot past the Hong Kong Jockey Club vet, a routine examination to which all runners in the international races were subjected.

Shortly afterwards Cazzy came in and said that the vet was unhappy with Ouija Board's action. Curious, we went out to see her trot by again, and there was indeed the merest hint of lameness. Ed's marvellous vet Mike Shepherd, who had ministered to her throughout her career, had travelled over on holiday to see her last race and now found himself on a busman's holiday:

he was asked to give his own opinion, while the duty farrier felt around the suspect area.

Throughout Ouija Board's career, Ed had handled her with skill, attention and dedication and had understood her so well, and at this moment his parallel understanding of how to handle her owners came into play. To get us out the way while she was examined further, he sent us off to breakfast.

By now I was becoming extremely anxious, and when at the breakfast – a cheerful communal affair – the American journalist Kathleen Donovan approached to ask about our horse's welfare I decided, for once in Ouija Board's career, that evasion was the appropriate action, and beetled back to the quarantine barn. Here I learned that an x-ray had confirmed that nothing was broken, but manual examination had shown that a splint in Ouija Board's leg – the same leg which had given her such trouble in the spring of 2005 – had suffered a very mild jarring: her leg was painful to the touch, and she had suffered a very slight swelling of the soft tissue.

It was entirely possible that she would be completely recovered by the following day and would still run her race, but to be on the safe side we asked the HKJC (who had issued a statement at noon announcing that she was lame and would be examined again in the morning) whether she could canter on the course in the afternoon. Extensive preparations for the track's flagship day would have had to be suspended while our horse was out on the track, but with characteristic energy Mark Player, who masterminds the Cathay Pacific International Races so brilliantly, swiftly made the necessary arrangements.

Under the watchful eye of Mike Shepherd, Jason cantered Ouija Board for about five furlongs round the all-weather track. She seemed to move easily enough, and when Jason pulled her up and returned towards us our optimism was restored. But after she had been cooling down for about 15 minutes she was trotted up again, and she was still slightly lame. Ed, standing with her a few yards away from the rest of the party, turned towards us and made the sign of cutting his throat. It was the end, and none of us standing in a desolate group out on the course made any pretence of masking our emotions. We hugged Ouija Board and we hugged each other, and the tears flowed and we were touched that Winfried Engelbrecht-Bresges, the CEO of the Hong Kong Jockey Club, came across to share this sad moment with us.

The tears were still flowing when we repaired to the bar of our hotel to come to terms with what had happened. But we had to break the news to the wider world, and we asked three journalists to join us: Lee Mottershead of the *Racing Post*, Julian Muscat of *The Times*, and Sean Magee, who was helping me with this book. Rather than rely on my hazy memory of the details of that emotional occasion I should offer Lee's own account published in the *Post*:

Tears and laughter, sadness and smiles. So many emotions and so many memories as nine of Ouija Board's most ardent fans – some involved in the story, some merely observers – sipped champagne and reminisced in a Hong Kong hotel lobby.

Ouija Board's last ever racecourse gallop – with Frankie Dettori under the towering apartment blocks at Sha Tin.

There was Lord Derby and wife Cazzy, Ed Dunlop and his better half Becky, Dunlop's vet Mike Shepherd and wife Camilla. Along with three hacks, they let day turn to night while discussing the object of their affections.

Evidence of what had gone on before was there for all to see on the face of Cazzy. The puffy eyes told the tale.

'We have changed the going at Sha Tin to soft with our tears,' she said. 'I haven't seen Teddy cry in ten years, but he wept in my arms today.'

They weren't alone. Even Hong Kong racing supremo Winfried Engelbrecht-Bresges was reported to have become moist around the eyes when joining the Ouija team for the moment when her racing career was deemed over.

Yes, this was to be the final stop in her first-career journey, one that has involved travelling more than 70,000 miles, competing in seven countries. Not that everyone wanted it to be the final stop.

'Hands up all those who think she should race at six,' asked the trainer. Five hands went up.

'I'd only race her if she was fit and well,' said Cazzy.

'But Duchess, I would never run her if she wasn't,' replied a determined Dunlop, adding another hand to his tally, yet fighting a lost cause.

On the subject of his 'darling girl' racing on at six, Lord Derby would not be moved.

Lady D. did, however, unilaterally announce the delaying of plans to send Ouija Board directly from Hong Kong to the US for covering by Kingmambo.

'I've made an executive decision,' she declared. 'She's not going to America yet. She needs to go back to her box at Ed's. When you're sick you want to be at home.'

'She'll be glad to get back home,' said Dunlop, before praising those who at home and abroad have looked after Ouija Board. And then he reflected.

'It's been such a long story with so many chapters,' he said. 'She's changed my life and done the same for the owner.

'When you're the trainer you're always looking forward and wanting to move on to the next race. Now it will be different. I will be able to look back and enjoy the memories.

'She was never going to be a Dessie or a Red Rum, but what she's done has made her the most popular Flat horse in the world. We must never forget it has all been about her.'

'She's kind of priceless,' added his wife.

Shortly before the impromptu party broke up, Cazzy disappeared, returning five minutes later with gift-wrapped presents for the three scribes, which when unwrapped turned out to be mousemats sporting a photograph of Ouija Board cruising past the post in the Prince of Wales's Stakes. I am reliably informed that the literary style of all three has been improved several pounds by the use of Ouija Board mousemats!

The rest of that evening was spent coming to terms with the fact that Ouija Board's racing career was indeed over, and we still felt very emotional on the following day when we went to Sha Tin for the Hong Kong International Races. Ouija Board's withdrawal had removed our own

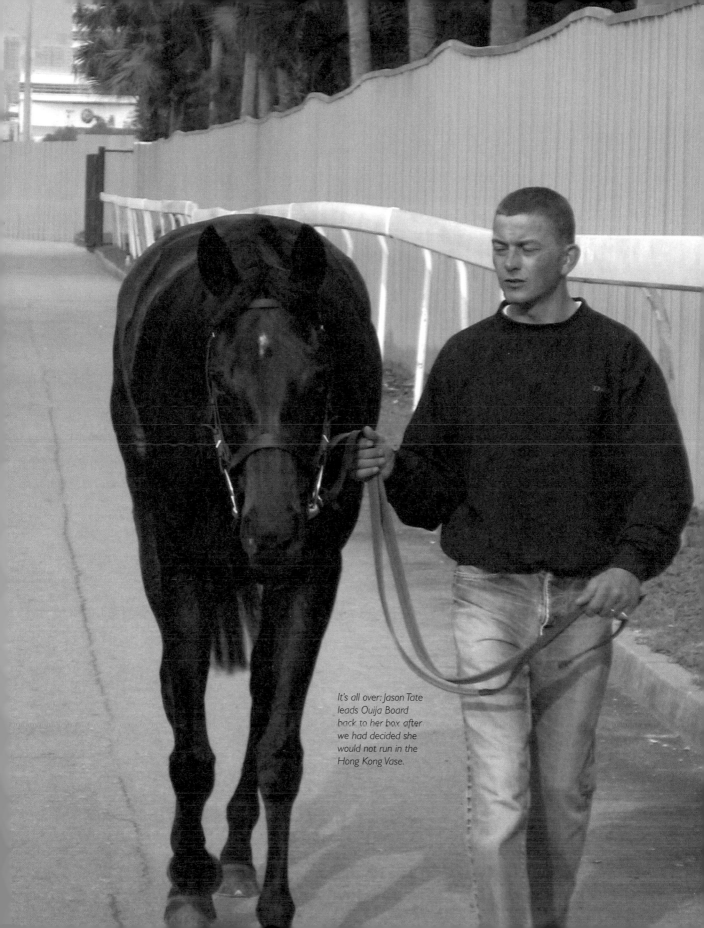

It's all over: Jason Tate leads Ouija Board back to her box after we had decided she would not run in the Hong Kong Vase.

involvement from the day, but there remained a programme of top-class racing – yet I was still asked for interviews about how she was, how we felt about her withdrawal, what would happen now, and so on. That level of interest just indicated to me the depth of affection which she now attracted wherever she went. Now it was all over.

None the less, we had a double reason to celebrate that evening – the career of our great mare, and the seventieth birthday of my stepfather Bill Spiegelberg the following day – and it was with a mixture of emotions that our party descended on the Cipriani restaurant.

In Ouija Board's absence the Hong Kong Vase was won by the eight-year-old gelding Collier Hill, who had won a 'bumper' – a National Hunt Flat Race – at Catterick in 2002 (and had been beaten by Ouija Board's half-brother Spectrometer at York the same year), and in 2006 had proved an unlikely hero of several big international races. So as the Ouija Board story was ending, another, as romantic in its own way, was reaching a fresh peak. Whether Ouija Board would have beaten Collier Hill was to me beside the point. In racing you have to play the hand you have been given, and with Ouija Board the cards had been snatched away at the eleventh hour.

After all the expectation and the emotion going into her final race, to have to leave Hong Kong without even having had a run was a terrible anti-climax and desperately disappointing. But Ouija Board was still in one piece. When asked about her withdrawal on the Saturday afternoon, Robin Trevor-Jones had observed: 'She's in her box today eating her food. If we had run her, she might not have been in her box this time tomorrow.' That was well put, and now we had the fresh and wonderfully exciting prospect of breeding from her.

Another thought struck me. We had been lucky that Ouija Board's splint had not played up at all during the 2006 season, which it could so easily have done. By now we were firmly decided that she would not race in 2007, and I am certain in my mind that the reappearance of the splint to prevent her running in Hong Kong was her way of telling us that enough was enough.

Having confirmed that she would be visiting Kingmambo in the spring, the plan had originally been that Ouija Board would go straight to Kentucky from Hong Kong. But as Cazzy had so wisely observed during that emotional session in the hotel bar, 'When you're sick you want to be at home.' So early the following week Ouija Board was flown back to Newmarket, and as usual started kicking the partition in the horsebox as soon as she sensed that she was nearly at Gainsborough Stables, which would be her home for only a few more weeks.

CHAPTER FIVE

'SHE'S TAKEN US ROUND THE WORLD AND CHANGED OUR LIVES'

Back at home, Ouija Board was let down gently. Her food intake was gradually reduced, spells on the horse-walker encouraged relaxation, and a daily session in the pool accelerated recovery. Early in January 2007 she left Gainsborough Stables for the last time and returned to the place of her birth, Stanley House Stud, where she continued the winding-down process, spending each morning turned out in a paddock and generally coming to terms with life away from the hothouse of the training stable.

Once it was confirmed that she was completely recovered from the niggle which had prevented her running in Hong Kong we made arrangements for her trip to Kingmambo in Kentucky, and on the evening of 6 February she was collected for her journey by Brian Taylor, yet again her travelling mentor, waved on her way by a collection of stud staff and sustained by a packet of strong mints sent up by her former groom Pat Evens.

It would be a long slog before Ouija Board settled into her new quarters in Kentucky. Three quarters of an hour to Stansted; a wait in the horsebox there while the paperwork was cleared; being transferred to her travelling stall and high-loaded into the plane; a seven-hour flight to Newark, New Jersey (during which, by extraordinary coincidence, she would be accompanied by her nephew Chess Board, a horse I had had in training with Sir Mark Prescott and had sold the previous summer); two hours in another horsebox to the quarantine clearance unit at Newburgh; then an overnight box trip of at least twelve hours, finally arriving at around 6 a.m. local time at Lane's End Farm.

The journey went without hitch, and in Kentucky yet another extraordinary coincidence awaited her, for her companion in the paddock she occupied while waiting to visit Kingmambo was none other than Film Maker, who had finished one place behind her in each of her three Breeders' Cup races.

At 7.30 a.m. on Monday 26 February Ouija Board was covered by Kingmambo, and four weeks later, to our great joy, she was scanned in foal.

While we awaited her return to Newmarket we were able to reflect on her extraordinary career.

The barest bones of the Ouija Board story are that she won ten of her twenty-two races, seven of her victories coming at Group 1 level; that she won two Classics and two Breeders' Cup races; that she raced in seven different countries on three continents, travelling around 75,000 miles in the process; that she amassed £3,510,682 in prize money, the second-largest amount ever won by a British-trained racehorse; and that she won more awards than any other racehorse. Indeed, the awards kept coming in after Ouija Board had ceased racing, with January 2007 bringing a second Eclipse Award as well as the thoroughly deserved stable staff award won by her mentor Chris Hinson.

I finish where I started, by saying that Ouija Board is an extraordinary horse but could not have done what she did without the equally

Back home at Stanley House Stud. My daughter Hetty Stanley (right) and her cousin Laura Murray pay their respects to Ouija Board shortly before her departure for Kentucky and her date with Kingmambo.

Chris Hinson receives his hugely deserved Stable Employee of the Year Award from Sir Peter O'Sullevan – with Brough Scott looking on – in February 2007.

extraordinary skill and dedication of so many people. I have tried to highlight their contributions in this book, from my brother Peter and Pat Cronin at the stud, to Ed, who has done such a remarkable job and kept a steady nerve throughout, Chris and all the team at Gainsborough. It has been a truly remarkable feat of training to have kept Ouija Board in such form for four years.

Ouija Board seemed to change the lives of the whole team.

At Gainsborough Stables, Ed declares that she was 'a once-in-a-lifetime experience, and I can only dream that I'll have another horse as good. Even were I to do so, I'll always be known as the trainer of Ouija Board. She's taken us round the world, and changed our lives.' For

Becky, 'It's been a privilege having her in the yard.' For Chris Hinson she was 'something very special indeed, an absolute star', for Steve Young 'a joy'. For Angela Lowe, 'It has been a truly fantastic honour to have been involved with such a wonderful horse as Ouija Board. It was a great experience for me to assist in her worldwide travel plans and I will always treasure the memories that she has given me.' And Robin Trevor-Jones, so often her companion on her overseas crusades, reflects that Ouija Board 'has given me some unbelievable memories and is by far the best racehorse I have ever had the privilege to take racing. I will miss her greatly and in my dreams I would be able to travel one as good as her in the future – but I doubt it!'

Brian Taylor, who did so much to make Ouija Board the seasoned imperturbable international jet-setter that she became, wrote to me after he had returned from taking her to Kentucky to meet Kingmambo: 'It has always been a great pleasure to be on every one of Ouija Board's flights. She was a model traveller – not too good on the road, but I have seen a lot worse than her over the years. In my experience, I have learnt that every great horse has a little quirk, and hers was travelling by road. Why? I still cannot figure that one out, and I do not think I ever will.'

Her regular vet Mike Shepherd has told me: 'Without a doubt Ouija Board is the best racehorse I have dealt with, and unfortunately am ever likely to deal with. Watching her win the English Oaks in the yard canteen with all the lads was spine-tingling, and the start of the most amazing few years. She was not without her share of problems, but she had an ability to respond well and quickly to treatment and move on without lingering issues.'

My family has been transformed in like manner. For my mother Rosie Spiegelberg, 'she has taken us to another planet.' For my brother Peter, in many ways the unsung hero of the Ouija Board story, 'She's been a once-in-a-lifetime experience for us all, and she'll be a dream mare to have at the stud in the future. I only hope she has a few daughters half as good as herself, to project her influence way into the decades ahead.' For Peter's wife Frances, 'Ouija Board has spoilt us forever. We have lived the dream for four years, going from Group 1 to Group 1 around the world. Will racing ever be the same again without her in the paddock?'

And no one has been more under the spell of Ouija Board than my wife Cazzy: 'How can I ever encapsulate what Ouija Board has meant to me personally in one sentence? After marrying into a racing dynasty I attended race meetings as a matter of course – and then she came along and lit up a passion that only a horse can. She has given us the highest highs (the Oaks, the two Breeders' Cups) and on occasion the lowest lows

Team Ouija at Churchill Downs, November 2006, with my stepfather Bill Spiegelberg and my mother Rosie on the left.

(her first Prince of Wales's Stakes at Royal Ascot at York, and her abortive trip for a second Hong Kong Vase), but with each race I became more addicted to the rush of adrenaline that always came two furlongs before the winning post. She is entirely responsible for getting me completely and utterly hooked on the racing and breeding of Thoroughbreds.'

Racing historians talk of the earlier greats among racemares in appropriately reverential tones: of how Sceptre won four of the five Classics (all bar the Derby) in 1902; of how Pretty Polly was so adored that when she was beaten in the 1906 Ascot Gold Cup, the *Sporting Life* made no pretence of impartiality and declared, 'Alas and again alas! Pretty Polly beaten!'; of how Petite Etoile enchanted the racing public half a century ago; and of how in more recent years the

Old rivals in the calm of a Kentucky paddock: Film Maker (right), who finished one place behind our heroine in each of their three Breeders' Cup Filly and Mare Turfs, and Ouija Board.

We commissioned Katie O'Sullivan to paint this portrait of Ouija Board winning the Oaks, copies of which hang at Knowsley, Stanley House Stud and Gainsborough Stables. A life-size bronze of Ouija Board by Emma McDermott will stand at Knowsley, with a half-size version at Stanley House Stud.

likes of Time Charter, Stanerra, Oh So Sharp, Pebbles, Triptych, Miesque (like Ouija Board a dual Breeders' Cup winner) and Bosra Sham have similarly captured hearts.

By the end of her career, Ouija Board had indisputably joined that elite band in the public affections. She took us all over the world, brought us excitement beyond our wildest dreams, and, very far from least, brought about a revival and renewal of the fortunes of the racing and breeding interests which have meant so much to so many generations of my family. Her retirement from the racecourse left a huge hole in our lives, but the prospect of rearing and racing her offspring heralds a new phase in the great Ouija Board adventure.

THE RECORD

Ouija Board's pedigree

bay filly, 6 March 2001

Cape Cross bay 1994	Green Desert	Danzig	Northern Dancer
			Pas de Nom
		Foreign Courier	Sir Ivor
			Courtly Dee
	Park Appeal	Ahonoora	Lorenzaccio
			Helen Nichols
		Balidaress	Balidar
			Innocence
Selection Board bay 1982	Welsh Pageant	Tudor Melody	Tudor Minstrel
			Matelda
		Picture Light	Court Martial
			Queen Of Light
	Ouija	Silly Season	Tom Fool
			Double Deal
		Samanda	Alycidon
			Gradisca

Bred by Stanley Estate & Stud Co. in England

Cape Cross

Won 5 of 19 races, inc. Lockinge S-Gr1, Queen Anne S.-Gr2, Goodwood Mile-Gr2. Also 2nd 3 times. 3rd 3 times and 4th 3 times. Big, strong, well-made type. High-class miler, notably game and consistent. Unraced beyond 9f (which he appeared to stay), effective on firm, good and good to soft ground. Well-bred. Half-brother to 4 winners, inc. Lord Of Appeal (Listed) and the dams of Kareymah (Gr3) and Diktat (Gr1). By a top-class sprinter-miler out of champion 2-y-o filly whose siblings include Gr1 winners Desirable (dam of Shadayid, Gr1) and Alydaress and Gr1-placed Nashamaa, plus the dams of Russian Rhythm and Bin Ajwaad. Stands at Kildangan Stud, Co. Kildare, Ireland, at a (2007) fee of €50,000.

Selection Board

Ran only twice, placed 2nd in Ayr maiden at 2, unplaced at 3. Plain, leggy, evidently less than sound. Well-bred. Sister to top-class miler Teleprompter, half-sister to Chatoyant (c by Rainbow Quest; Gr3), Message Pad (c by Rousillon; Gr3-placed) and Rosia Bay (f by Blakeney; winner, dam of Gr1 winners Ibn Bey and Roseate Tern). Dam of: Officer Cadet (1987 c by Shernazar; winner), Draft Board (1989 f by Rainbow Quest; winner), Star Selection (1991 g by Rainbow Quest; Listed-placed winner), Pass Mark (1992 f by Never So Bold; placed), Cruinn A Bhord (1995 f by Inchinor; winner), Victor Ludorum (1996 f by Rainbow Quest, unraced), Spectrometer (1997 c by Rainbow Quest; winner), unnamed (1998 g by Rainbow Quest; unraced), Coalition (1999 g by Polish Precedent; winner), Ouija Board (2001 f by Cape Cross; Oaks winner), Illuminatia (2002 g by Inchinor; unplaced). Died in 2002.

Ouija Board's career in summary

Left to right: date; course; race name and, in parentheses, status (1 = Group 1 race, 3 = Group 3 race, L = Listed Race); distance in furlongs; jockey; starting price or (where marked with *) local pari-mutuel return; finishing position; prize money won by Ouija Board in £ sterling or at the prevailing exchange rate.

2003

Date	Course	Race	Dist	Jockey	SP	Pos	Prize
3 Oct	Newmarket	Beech House Maiden Stakes	7	E Ahern	20-1	3rd	£1,098.00
21 Oct	Yarmouth	EBF Novice Stakes	7	J Spencer	EvensF	WON	£3,740.75
1 Nov	Newmarket	Montrose Stakes (L)	8	J Spencer	11-4F	3rd	£2,200.00

Season's total £7,038.75

2004

Date	Course	Race	Dist	Jockey	SP	Pos	Prize
2 May	Newmarket	Pretty Polly Stakes (L)	10	K Fallon	2-1F	WON	£17,400.00
4 June	Epsom Downs	Oaks Stakes (1)	12	K Fallon	7-2	WON	£203,000.00
18 July	The Curragh	Irish Oaks (1)	12	K Fallon	4-7F	WON	£167,042.25
3 Oct	Longchamp	Prix de l'Arc de Triomphe (1)	12	J Murtagh	9-1*	3rd	£128,789.00
30 Oct	Lone Star Park	Breeders' Cup Filly & Mare Turf (1)	11	K Fallon	9-10F*	WON	£409,609.00

Season's total £925,840.25

2005

Date	Course	Race	Dist	Jockey	SP	Pos	Prize
15 June	York	Prince of Wales's Stakes (1)	10	J Spencer	7-2	7th	—
24 Sept	Newmarket	Princess Royal Stakes (3)	12	L Dettori	11-8F	WON	£23,200.00
29 Oct	Belmont Park	Breeders' Cup Filly & Mare Turf (1)	10	J Bailey	23-10F*	2nd	£110,417.00
27 Nov	Tokyo	Japan Cup (1)	12	K Fallon	118-10*	5th	£127,078.00
11 Dec	Sha Tin	Hong Kong Vase (1)	12	K Fallon	69-20*	WON	£536,193.00

Season's total £796,888.00

2006

Date	Course	Race	Dist	Jockey	SP	Pos	Prize
25 March	Nad Al Sheba	Sheema Classic (1)	12	K Fallon	9-4F	4th	£145,348.84
23 April	Sha Tin	Queen Elizabeth II Cup (1)	10	L Dettori	8-5F*	3rd	£112,697.00
2 June	Epsom Downs	Coronation Cup (1)	12	L Dettori	11-4	2nd	£53,800.00
21 June	Ascot	Prince of Wales's Stakes (1)	10	O Peslier	8-1	WON	£211,207.40
8 July	Sandown Park	Eclipse Stakes (1)	10	C Soumillon	2-1F	5th	£12,347.10
5 Aug	Goodwood	Nassau Stakes (1)	10	L Dettori	EvensF	WON	£113,560.00
9 Sept	Leopardstown	Irish Champion Stakes (1)	10	J Spencer	11-4	2nd	£130,344.83
4 Nov	Churchill Downs	Breeders' Cup Filly & Mare Turf (1)	11	L Dettori	14-10F*	WON	£690,698.00
26 Nov	Tokyo	Japan Cup (1)	12	L Dettori	17-2*	3rd	£310,912.00

Season's total £1,780,915.17

Career total place money £1,135,031.77
Career total win money £2,375,650.40
Career total winnings £3,510,682.17

The main statistics

Ouija Board

- ran in 22 races, winning 10
- won seven races at Group 1 level: Oaks, Irish Oaks and Breeders' Cup Filly and Mare Turf in 2004; Hong Kong Vase in 2005; Prince of Wales's Stakes, Nassau Stakes and Breeders' Cup Filly and Mare Turf in 2006
- was second only to Allez France, who won eight Group 1 races, in Group 1 victories by a filly/mare
- ran in 18 Group 1 races in all: of her 19 races between the 2004 Oaks and 2006 Japan Cup exclusive, only one – the Princess Royal Stakes – was not a Group 1 contest
- finished runner-up three times, third five times, fourth once and unplaced three times
- won £3,510,682 in overall prize money, a total for an English-trained horse bettered only by Singspiel between 1994 and 1997
- won £2,375,650 in win prize money
- failed to collect any prize money on only one occasion, when seventh in the 2005 Prince of Wales's Stakes at York
- was ridden in her career by eight different jockeys: Kieren Fallon (seven rides, five wins), Frankie Dettori (six rides, three wins), Jamie Spencer (four rides, one win), Olivier Peslier (one ride, one win), Johnny Murtagh (one ride), Eddie Ahern (one ride), Jerry Bailey (one ride) and Christophe Soumillon (one ride)
- ran in seven different countries: eleven races in England (winning six), three in the USA (winning two), two in Hong Kong (winning one), two in Ireland (winning one), two in Japan, one in France and one in Dubai
- travelled 73,923 miles by plane on 26 individual flights and spent approximately 160 hours in the air (figures supplied by her devoted flying groom Brian Taylor)
- raced at sixteen different racecourses: Newmarket (four races, two wins), Epsom Downs (two races, one win), Sha Tin (two races, one win), Fuchu [Tokyo] (two races), The Curragh (one race, one win), Ascot (one race, one win), Goodwood (one race, one win), Lone Star Park (one race, one win), Churchill Downs (one race, one win), Yarmouth (one race, one win), Belmont Park (one race), Leopardstown (one race), Longchamp (one race), Sandown Park (one race), Nad Al Sheba (one race), York (one race)
- recorded her longest winning distance when winning the 2004 Oaks by seven lengths from All Too Beautiful
- recorded her shortest winning distance when winning the 2006 Nassau Stakes by a short head from Alexander Goldrun
- started favourite in 12 of her 22 races
- returned her longest winning SP in the 2006 Prince of Wales's Stakes: 8-1
- returned her shortest winning SP in the 2004 Irish Oaks: 4-7

Awards

Ouija Board's career brought a plethora of major racing industry awards to her and her connections. They are:

2004

Cartier Awards
Three-Year-Old Filly of the Year: Ouija Board
Horse of the Year: Ouija Board
Racehorse Owners' Association Awards
Outstanding Three-Year-Old Filly of the Year: Ouija Board
Owner of the Year: Lord Derby
Derby Awards of the Horserace Writers' and Photographers' Association
Owner of the Year: Lord Derby
International Trainer of the Year: Ed Dunlop
Thoroughbred Breeders' Association Awards
Breeder of the Year: Stanley House Stud
British Horseracing Board Awards
Horse of the Year: Ouija Board
Three-Year-Old Filly of the Year: Ouija Board
Eclipse Awards (USA)
Filly and Mare Turf Specialist: Ouija Board
Breeders' Cup Breeders Awards (USA)
Breeder of Filly and Mare Turf winner: Stanley House Stud

2006

Cartier Awards
Horse of the Year: Ouija Board
Older Horse of the Year: Ouija Board
Racehorse Owners' Association Awards
Horse of the Year: Ouija Board
Older Horse of the Year: Ouija Board
Owner of the Year: Lord Derby
Thoroughbred Breeders' Association Awards
TBA Silver Salver for special merit: Stanley House Stud
Eclipse Awards (USA)
Filly and Mare Turf Specialist: Ouija Board
Breeders' Cup Breeders Awards (USA)
Breeder of Filly and Mare Turf winner: Stanley House Stud
Stud and Stable Staff Awards
Stable Employee of the Year: Chris Hinson
Senior Staff Award: Chris Hinson
Irish Thoroughbred Breeders' Association
Overseas Breeder of the Year: Lord Derby

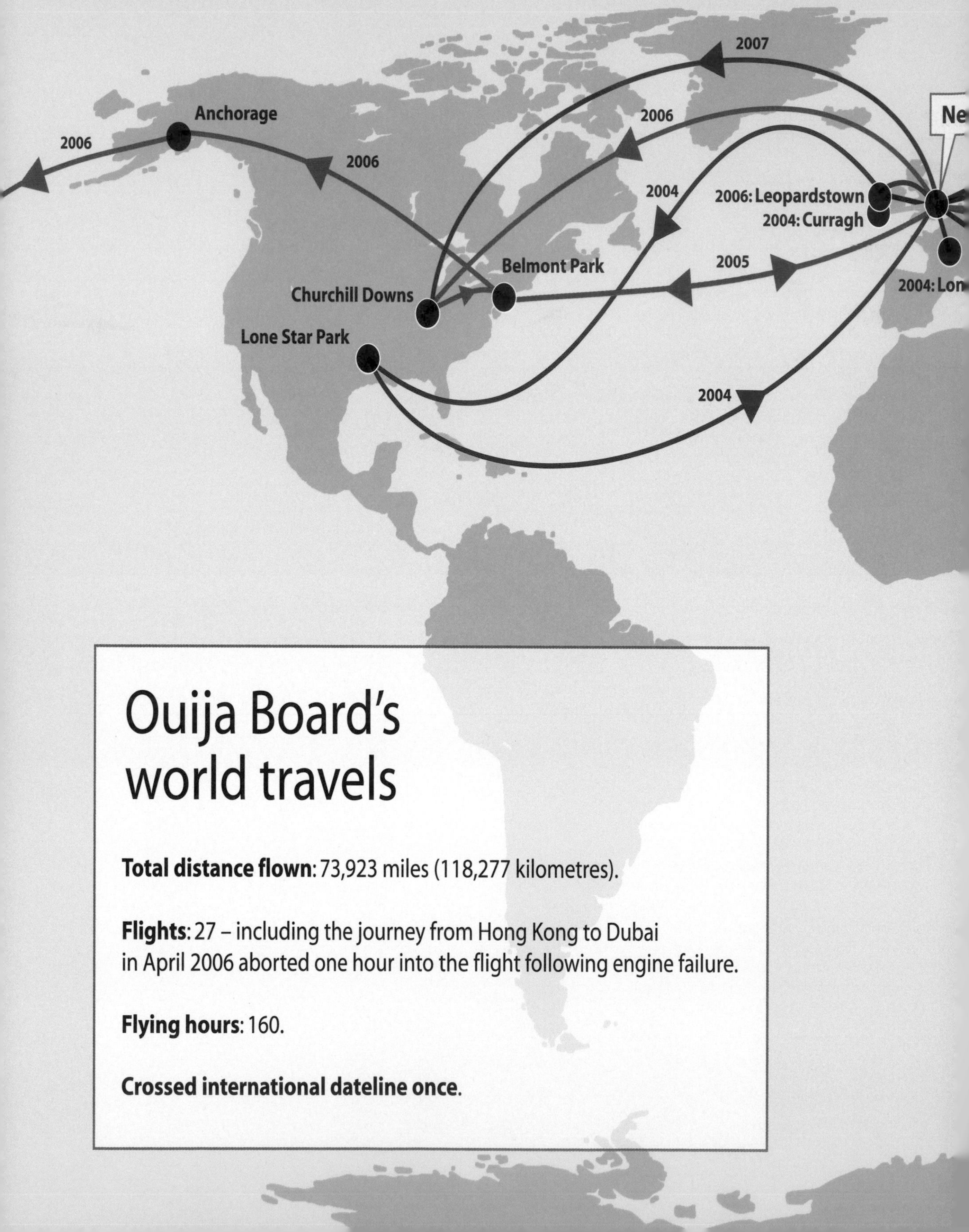

2007

2006

Anchorage

2006

2006

2004

2006: Leopardstown
2004: Curragh

Ne[w]

Churchill Downs

Belmont Park

2005

2004

Lone Star Park

2004: Lon[

2004

Ouija Board's world travels

Total distance flown: 73,923 miles (118,277 kilometres).

Flights: 27 – including the journey from Hong Kong to Dubai in April 2006 aborted one hour into the flight following engine failure.

Flying hours: 160.

Crossed international dateline once.

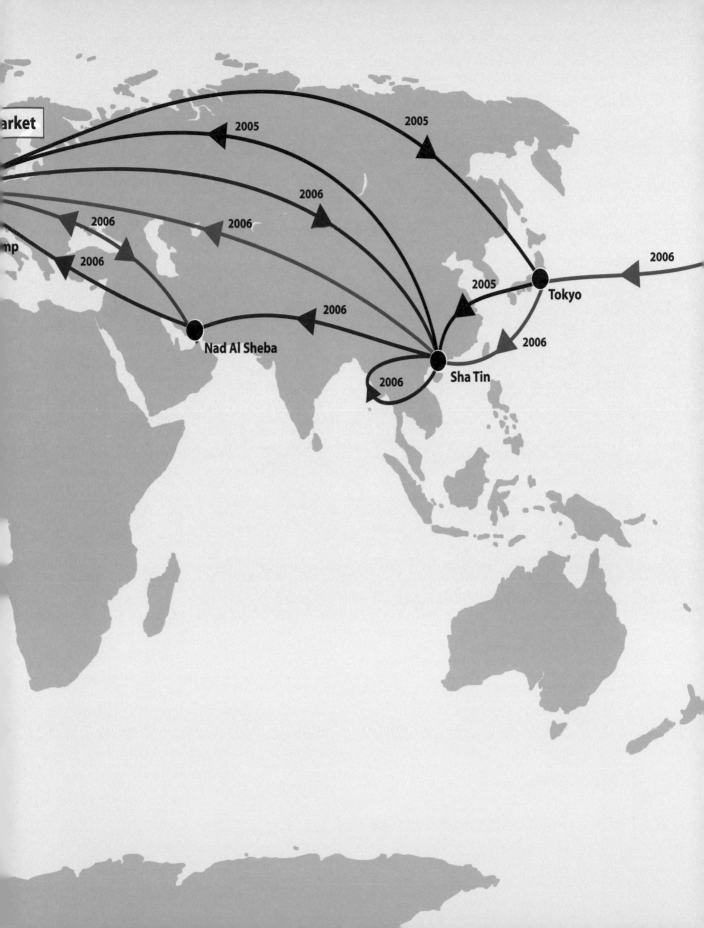

Ouija Board's career race by race

Full results of Ouija Board's twenty-two races are here taken from the returns in the *Racing Post*, with Official Ratings (OR), Topspeed ratings (TS) and *Racing Post* Ratings (RPR) given where appropriate, along with the total starting price percentages (TOTAL SP). Starting prices given for races in France, the USA, Hong Kong and Dubai are so-called 'industry prices'. Where appropriate, the time for each race is compared with the course average. The Analysis comments were not given for all international races.

NEWMARKET

03 October 2003

Good To Firm

1:10 Beech House Stud EBF Maiden Stakes (Class D) (Class 4) (2yo) 7f

[off 1:13] £7,137.00, £2,196.00, £1,098.00, £549.00

			Draw	TRAINER	Age	Wgt	JOCKEY	SP	OR	TS	RPR
1		Secret Charm (IRE)	7	B W Hills	2	8-9	Michael Hills	11/2		70	78+
2	nk	Gravardlax (GB)	21	B J Meehan	2	9-0	Pat Eddery	5/1		75	82
3	1¼	Ouija Board	17	E A L Dunlop	2	8-9	Eddie Ahern	20/1		66	74+
4	1½	Meneef (USA)	11	M P Tregoning	2	9-0	R Hills	8/1		66	75+
5	¾	Slavonic (USA)	10	J H M Gosden	2	9-0	Richard Hughes	14/1		64	73+
6	hd	Mr Tambourine Man	12	P F I Cole	2	9-0	L Dettori	4/1F		64	73
7	shd	Obay	18	E A L Dunlop	2	9-0	Darryll Holland	33/1		64	73+
8	½	Ali Deo (GB)	16	W J Haggas	2	9-0	Oscar Urbina	33/1		62	71+
9	1½	Thirteen Tricks (USA)	1	Mrs A J Perrett	2	8-9	M J Kinane	14/1		52	63+
10	nk	Moscow Times	22	D R C Elsworth	2	8-9	Nicky Mackay(5)	9/1		57	67+
11	1½	Landucci	3	J W Hills	2	9-0	John Egan	25/1		52	63+
12	3	Mission Man	23	R Hannon	2	9-0	Jamie Spencer	25/1		43	56+
13	1¼	Bluefield (IRE)	20	R F Johnson Houghton	2	9-0	Adrian T Nicholls	66/1		39	52
14	1½	Pagan Magic (USA)	19	J A R Toller	2	9-0	Joe Fanning	25/1		34	49
15	hd	Ellina (GB)	15	Mrs Lydia Pearce	2	8-9	Russell Price	66/1		29	43
16	1¼	Strider	4	Sir Michael Stoute	2	9-0	K Dalgleish	40/1		30	45
17	nk	Arrgatt (IRE)	5	M A Jarvis	2	9-0	Philip Robinson	16/1		30	44
18	shd	Maluti (GB)	9	Rae Guest	2	9-0	Jamie Mackay	100/1		30	44
19	hd	Star Pupil	13	A M Balding	2	9-0	Martin Dwyer	40/1		30	44
20	½	Dalisay (IRE)	24	Sir Michael Stoute	2	8-9	K Fallon	10/1		23	37
21	½	Chaayid (IRE)	2	J L Dunlop	2	9-0	Ted Durcan	50/1		—	41
22	nk	Wyoming	8	J A R Toller	2	8-9	Dale Gibson	66/1		—	35
23	26	Desert Diplomat (IRE)	6	Sir Michael Stoute	2	9-0	Fergal Lynch	20/1		—	—

23 ran TIME 1m 25.77s (slow by 2.67s) **TOTAL SP** 140%

OUIJA BOARD benefited from racing against the far rail and she momentarily looked the likely winner into the final two furlongs. She kept on well and looks the type to go on next season.

YARMOUTH

21 October 2003

Good To Firm

2:50 European Breeders Fund Novice Stakes (Class D) (Class 4) (2yo) (7f3y) 7f

[off 2:50] £3,740.75, £1,151.00, £575.50, £287.75

		Draw	TRAINER	Age	Wgt	JOCKEY	SP	OR	TS	RPR
1		Ouija Board	5	E A L Dunlop	2	8-7	Jamie Spencer	EvensF		45	91+
2	4	Rydal (USA)	2	G A Butler	2	8-12	Eddie Ahern	11/4	83	38	84
3	2	Naaddey	4	M R Channon	2	9-2 v1	Sam Hitchcott(3)	5/1	92	39	86+
4	2	Ticero (GB)	3	C E Brittain	2	8-12	Seb Sanders	20/1		26	74
5	5	Stanley Crane (USA)	6	B Hanbury	2	8-12 t	R Hills	12/1		—	62
6	1	Go Yellow	7	P D Evans	2	8-12	N Callan	20/1	82	—	59

6 ran TIME 1m 28.02s (slow by 4.02s) **TOTAL SP** 110%

This was quite a decent event for the time of the year and OUIJA BOARD put up an impressive display on ground that had been watered overnight and had the further benefit of the morning showers. Once again the runners came up the centre of the course but the daughter of Cape Cross was ridden with any amount of confidence and was nicely anchored by Jamie Spencer as the other five runners went along at a reasonable pace. However, once brought with her effort over a furlong out she showed a sparkling turn of foot to win decisively. She was still green and hung left when hitting the front but looks sure to win in decent company next year.

NEWMARKET

01 November 2003

Good To Soft

3:30 EBF Montrose Fillies' Stakes (Class A) (Listed Race) (Class 1) (2yo) 1m

[off 3:33] £11,600.00, £4,400.00, £2,200.00, £1,000.00, £500.00, £300.00

		Draw	TRAINER	Age	Wgt	JOCKEY	SP	OR	TS	RPR
1		Spotlight	7	J L Dunlop	2	8-8	Pat Eddery	7/2	98	88	101
2	4	St Francis Wood	4	J Noseda	2	8-9 1	L Dettori	7/1		77	93
3	shd	Ouija Board	8	E A L Dunlop	2	8-8	Jamie Spencer	11/4F		76	92
4	1	Kelucia (IRE)	10	J S Goldie	2	8-8	Royston Ffrench	6/1	100	73	90
5	2	Cusco (IRE)	5	R Hannon	2	8-8	Pat Dobbs	66/1	86	67	85
6	hd	Shalaya (IRE)	12	Sir Michael Stoute	2	8-8	K Fallon	10/1		67	85
7	hd	Saffron Fox	3	J G Portman	2	8-8	Steve Drowne	25/1	87	67	85
8	½	Crystal (IRE)	1	B J Meehan	2	8-8	Michael Hills	25/1		65	83
9	½	Maganda (IRE)	6	M A Jarvis	2	8-8	Philip Robinson	9/1		63	82
10	hd	Mango Mischief (IRE)	9	J L Dunlop	2	8-8	Seb Sanders	20/1		63	82
11	5	Baileys Dancer (GB)	2	M Johnston	2	8-8	Joe Fanning	14/1	90	48	71
12	3	Lady Georgina	11	J R Fanshawe	2	8-8 t	Martin Dwyer	33/1	80	39	64

12 ran TIME 1m 38.59s (slow by 2.59s) **TOTAL SP** 118%

OUIJA BOARD had won her maiden at Yarmouth in impressive style and ran another sound race as she was switched to the outside and just didn't have the finishing kick to tackle the winner. She remains a nice prospect.

NEWMARKET

02 May 2004
Good

3:50   R. L. Davison Pretty Polly Stakes (Class A) (Listed Race) (Fillies) (Class 1) (3yo) 1m2f

[off 3:53]£17,400.00, £6,600.00, £3,300.00, £1,500.00, £750.00, £450.00

			Draw	TRAINER	Age	Wgt	JOCKEY	SP	OR	TS	RPR
1		Ouija Board	4	E A L Dunlop	3	8-8	K Fallon	2/1F	93	81	111+
2	6	Sahool (GB)	6	M P Tregoning	3	8-8	R Hills	13/2	86	69	100
3	½	Rave Reviews (IRE)	8	J L Dunlop	3	8-8	M J Kinane	16/1	81	68	99
4	1¼	Brindisi (GB)	2	B W Hills	3	8-8	Michael Hills	12/1		65	97
5	½	Kisses For Me (IRE)	9	A P O'Brien	3	8-9 1	J Murtagh	5/1		64	97
6	11	Opera Comique (FR)	7	Saeed Bin Suroor	3	8-8 t	L Dettori	7/2		41	75
7	1¾	Lady Peaches	5	D Mullarkey	3	8-8	Joe Fanning	100/1		37	72
8	5	Rendezvous Point (USA)	1	J H M Gosden	3	8-8	K Darley	16/1		27	62
PU		He Jaa (IRE)	3	C E Brittain	3	8-8	Darryll Holland	20/1		—	—

9 ran TIME 2m 2.92s (slow by 1.42s)   **TOTAL SP** 110%

Brindisi made sure this was a stamina test, resulting in a noteworthy time recorded by runaway winner OUIJA BOARD. While the overall form can be questioned at this level, OUIJA BOARD, whose dam is a sister to that late developer Teleprompter, looks a Group performer. Her debut third to Secret Charm looks better after that filly's unlucky run in the Guineas. Whether she quite deserved the flattering quotes for the Oaks on the bare form is debatable – the Ladbrokes quote of 20-1 seemed fair, if not tempting – and it is arguable that ten furlongs looks her optimum trip on breeding. While the weakening Brindisi flattered the winner's swoop to glory, she was value for more than the impressive six lengths and she could take all the beating in the Musidora if connections took that route to the Oaks.

EPSOM

04 June 2004

Good

4:10 Vodafone Oaks (Class A) (Group 1) (Fillies) (Class 1) (3yo) (1m4f10y) 1m4f

[off 4:10]£203,000.00, £77,000.00, £38,500.00, £17,500.00, £8,750.00, £5,250.00

			Draw	TRAINER	Age	Wgt	JOCKEY	SP	OR	TS	RPR
1		Ouija Board	3	E A L Dunlop	3	9-0	K Fallon	7/2	110	120	124
2	7	All Too Beautiful (IRE)	6	A P O'Brien	3	9-0	Jamie Spencer	11/4F		106	113
3	3½	Punctilious	2	Saeed Bin Suroor	3	9-0 t	L Dettori	100/30	110	99	108
4	1½	Necklace (GB)	5	A P O'Brien	3	9-0	J Murtagh	10/1		96	105
5	18	Crystal (IRE)	7	B J Meehan	3	9-0	Michael Hills	25/1	93	60	76
6	4	Sundrop (JPN)	4	Saeed Bin Suroor	3	9-0	Kerrin McEvoy	3/1	117	52	70
7	dist	Kisses For Me (IRE)	1	A P O'Brien	3	9-0	P J Scallan	66/1		—	—

7 ran TIME 2m 35.41s (fast by 0.59s)   TOTAL SP 111%

A disappointing turnout and the dismal showing of 1,000 Guineas runner-up Sundrop should not detract from another scintillating performance from OUIJA BOARD, who spreadeagled her rivals in leading home distances that would have done justice to a three-mile chase. Ouija Board settled any arguments about her stamina and recorded a time faster than the Coronation Cup despite the small field. She will need to be supplemented for the Irish Oaks, which was mentioned as a possible target. There look to be plenty of others for this talented filly, who was clearly the only genuine 12-furlong Group 1 performer on view. Her Pretty Polly win had been visually impressive and she certainly has the speed to swamp her rivals over that ten furlongs, which naturally adds the Nassau Stakes to her potential targets. While that is the natural order of things, it would be lovely to see her considered for the Coral-Eclipse against her elders and the colts (the sponsors obviously respect her as she was given an 8-1 quote) as the mile-and-a-half Classics have lost their lustre in recent years. Ouija Board did not look happy around Tattenham Corner but was back on the bridle as others committed early in the straight and she passed them as if they were standing still to burst clear as she had done at Newmarket. She has left her two-year-old form well behind and is improving at a rate of knots – she went into the Pretty Polly rated only 93 – and if she proves as progressive as some of her relatives, including Teleprompter, there are exciting times ahead for her connections and she could take some beating at the Breeders' Cup Filly and Mare turf as she has been campaigned lightly to date but her family are tough.

CURRAGH

18 July 2004

Good To Firm

4:15 Darley Irish Oaks (Group 1) (Fillies) (3yo) 1m4f

[off 4:15]£167,042.25, £54,366.20, £26,197.18, £9,295.77, £6,478.87, £3,661.97, £845.07, £845.07

			Draw	TRAINER	Age	Wgt	JOCKEY	SP	OR	TS	RPR
1		Ouija Board (GB)	4	E A L Dunlop	3	9-0	K Fallon	4/7F		117	117
2	1	Punctilious (GB)	6	Saeed Bin Suroor	3	9-0 t	L Dettori	5/1		115	114
3	¾	Hazarista (IRE)	5	John M Oxx	3	9-0	M J Kinane	20/1	100	114	113
4	7	All Too Beautiful	7	A P O'Brien	3	9-0	Jamie Spencer	4/1	110	103	102
5	4	Marinnette (IRE)	1	M P Sunderland	3	9-0	J A Heffernan	200/1	79	97	95?
6	4	Danelissima	3	J S Bolger	3	9-0 b	K J Manning	16/1	105	90	89
7	4	Royal Tigress (USA)	2	A P O'Brien	3	9-0 b1	C O'Donoghue	50/1	105	—	83

7 ran TIME 2m 28.20s (fast by 2.80s)   TOTAL SP 113%

This may have lacked the visual splendour of her Epsom triumph, but it takes a very smart fillly to complete the Oaks double, and OUIJA BOARD rose to the occasion in stylish fashion. With only seven in the line-up there was a chance that this could turn into a tactical affair, but there were no legitimate excuses after Ouija Board had asserted from around a furlong and a half down to win with more than the official margin to spare. The Nassau Stakes comes up too soon, so the choice for her next race would seem to lie between the Yorkshire Oaks and the Juddmonte International. With owner Lord Derby expressing the view that ten furlongs may be her optimum trip the latter must be favourite. In any case, she has proved herself over a mile and a half on the two days that really mattered, and Ed Dunlop has done a marvellous job to exploit her talent to the full in recent months.

03 October 2004

Good

4:30   Prix de l'Arc de Triomphe Lucien Barriere (Group 1) (Entire Colts & Fillies) (3yo+) 1m4f

[off 4:31]£643,831.00, £257,577.00, £128,789.00, £64,338.00, £32,225.00

			Draw	TRAINER	Age	Wgt	JOCKEY	SP	OR	TS	RPR
1		Bago	5	J E Pease	3	8-11	T Gillet	10/1		130	129
2	½	Cherry Mix (FR)	1	A Fabre	3	8-11	C Soumillon	33/1		129	128
3	1	Ouija Board (GB)	9	E A L Dunlop	3	8-8	J Murtagh	7/1		124	123+
4	2	Acropolis (IRE)	19	A P O'Brien	3	8-11	Jamie Spencer	100/1		123	123
5	shd	North Light (IRE)	12	Sir Michael Stoute	3	8-11	K Fallon	9/2F		122	123
6	½	Vallee Enchantee (IRE)	16	E Lellouche	4	9-2	S Pasquier	14/1		119	120+
7	snk	Latice (IRE)	13	J-M Beguigne	3	8-8	M J Kinane	28/1		116	121+
8	2½	Silverskaya (USA)	6	J-C Rouget	3	8-8	I Mendizabal	66/1		111	115+
9	½	Warrsan (IRE)	8	C E Brittain	6	9-5	Kerrin McEvoy	9/1		113	118
10	shd	Valixir (IRE)	20	A Fabre	3	8-11	E Legrix	9/1		112	117
11	nk	Execute (FR)	17	J E Hammond	7	9-5	D Boeuf	66/1		111	117
12	½	Blue Canari (FR)	3	P Bary	3	8-11	C-P Lemaire	40/1		110	118+
13	½	Pride	10	A De Royer-Dupre	4	9-2	T Jarnet	33/1		107	113
14	snk	Imperial Dancer (GB)	15	M R Channon	6	9-5	Ted Durcan	100/1		110	115
15	hd	Mamool (IRE)	14	Saeed Bin Suroor	5	9-5	L Dettori	11/1		109	115
16	½	Prospect Park	2	C Laffon-Parias	3	8-11	O Peslier	10/1		107	113
17	8	Tap Dance City	18	S Sasaki	7	9-5	T Sato	10/1		94	102
18	1½	Grey Swallow (IRE)	11	D K Weld	3	8-11	P J Smullen	5/1		90	98
19	10	Policy Maker (IRE)	4	E Lellouche	4	9-5	T Thulliez	131/10		74	83

19 ran TIME 2m 25.00s (fast by 6.50s)   **TOTAL SP** 133%

If there was an unlucky loser it was OUIJA BOARD. She was shuffled back in the big field and had to wait for a gap so that she was well adrift when starting to make her move. She did very well to get into contention on the outside but then could find no extra close home as the effort of getting into the race took its toll. She confirmed the impression created in the Oaks and Irish Oaks that she is a top-notch mile-and-a-half filly, well up to beating the colts, and she will be a four-year-old to look forward to.

LONE STAR PARK

30 October 2004

Yielding

8:45   Alberto VO5 Breeders' Cup Filly & Mare Turf (Grade 1) (Fillies & Mares) (3yo+) 1m3f

[off 8:48]£409,609.00, £157,542.00, £86,648.00, £44,899.00, £23,631.00

			Draw	TRAINER	Age	Wgt	JOCKEY	SP	OR	TS	RPR
1		Ouija Board (GB)	5	E A L Dunlop	3	8-6	K Fallon	10/11F		—	121
2	1½	Film Maker (USA)	3	H G Motion	4	8-11 b	J R Velazquez	20/1		—	117
3	nk	Wonder Again	12	James J Toner	5	8-11	F Prado	12/1		—	117
4	2¾	Moscow Burning	4	J Cassidy	4	8-11	J Valdivia Jr	20/1		—	113
5	1¼	Yesterday (IRE)	11	A P O'Brien	4	8-11 v	Jamie Spencer	8/1		—	111
6	1	Shaconage	6	M Shirota	4	8-11	R Bejarano	50/1		—	109
7	¾	Light Jig (GB)	7	R J Frankel	4	8-11	R Douglas	5/1		—	10
8	½	Riskaverse	9	Patrick J Kelly	5	8-11	C Velasquez	12/1		—	107
9	1	Super Brand (SAF)	1	K McLaughlin	5	8-10	P Day	33/1		—	104
10	5½	Katdogawn (GB)	2	J Cassidy	4	8-11	K Desormeaux	40/1		—	97
11	1	Megahertz (GB)	10	R J Frankel	5	8-11	C Nakatani	11/1		—	95
12	nk	Aubonne (GER)	8	E Libaud	4	8-11	J D Bailey	18/1		—	95

12 ran TIME 2m 18.25s   **TOTAL SP** 126%

YORK

15 June 2005

Good To Firm

3:45   Prince of Wales's Stakes (Group 1) (Class 1) (4yo+) (1m2f88y) 1m2½f

[off 3:46]£203,000.00, £77,000.00, £38,500.00, £17,500.00, £8,750.00, £5,250.00

			Draw	TRAINER	Age	Wgt	JOCKEY	SP	OR	TS	RPR
1		Azamour (IRE)	3	John M Oxx	4	9-0	M J Kinane	11/8F		120	127
2	1½	Ace (IRE)	6	A P O'Brien	4	9-0	K Fallon	7/1		117	124
3	5	Elvstroem (AUS)	5	T Vasil	5	9-0 t	Nash Rawiller	11/1		107	115
4	4	Touch Of Land	4	H-A Pantall	5	9-0	C-P Lemaire	12/1		99	107
5	5	Warrsan (IRE)	8	C E Brittain	7	9-0	Darryll Holland	14/1	120	89	98
6	5	Norse Dancer (IRE)	1	D R C Elsworth	5	9-0	John Egan	8/1	121	79	88
7	9	Ouija Board	2	E A L Dunlop	4	8-11	Jamie Spencer	7/2		58	68
8	1¼	Hazyview (GB)	7	N A Callaghan	4	9-0 v	Eddie Ahern	33/1	108	58	69

8 ran TIME 2m 8.15s (fast by 1.15s)   **TOTAL SP** 113%

OUIJA BOARD looked on very good terms with herself but unfortunately her chance was severely compromised when she lost the shoe from her right-hand fore – the hoof which had suffered a quarter crack – in the early stages, for Jamie Spencer reported that she kept getting unbalanced thereafter. She was in trouble early in the straight, and eventually came home in her own time. Her belated start to a season that promised so much therefore started inauspiciously, but Ed Dunlop reported that she had pulled up sound and he is hopeful no damage had been done. A good moving filly, she can be seen to better advantage back on a sound surface if all is well with her.

NEWMARKET

24 September 2005

Good

2:00 Princess Royal John Doyle Stakes (Group 3) (Fillies & Mares) (Class 1) (3yo+) 1m4f

[off 2:03]£23,200.00, £8,800.00, £4,400.00, £2,000.00, £1,000.00, £600.00

			Draw	TRAINER	Age	Wgt	JOCKEY	SP	OR	TS	RPR
1		Ouija Board	4	E A L Dunlop	4	9-0	L Dettori	11/8F	120	78	111
2	2½	Briolette (IRE)	14	A P O'Brien	3	8-6	K Fallon	8/1		74	107
3	1	Asawer	12	Sir Michael Stoute	3	8-6	R Hills	16/1	102	73	105
4	shd	Art Eyes (USA)	13	D R C Elsworth	3	8-6	Philip Robinson	12/1	100	73	105+
5	1½	Autumn Wealth (IRE)	1	Mrs A J Perrett	4	9-0	Shane Kelly	16/1	102	70	102
6	5	Polar Jem	11	G G Margarson	5	9-0	Adrian McCarthy	33/1	99	62	94
7	1¾	Mango Mischief (IRE)	6	J L Dunlop	4	9-3	Jamie Spencer	10/1	103	62	95
8	7	Miss Provvidence (IRE)	7	W R Swinburn	3	8-6	Eddie Ahern	12/1	85	48	80
9	¾	Alumni	5	B W Hills	3	8-6	Richard Hughes	16/1	106	47	79
10	½	Play Me	9	P W Chapple-Hyam	3	8-6	Alan Munro	50/1		46	78
11	2½	Rave Reviews (IRE)	15	J L Dunlop	4	9-0 b1	Ted Durcan	25/1	100	42	74
12	3½	Right Key (IRE)	10	Kevin Prendergast	3	8-9 v1	D P McDonogh	8/1		39	72
13	10	Higher Love (IRE)	2	M L W Bell	3	8-6	Joe Fanning	50/1	95	19	53

13 ran TIME 2m 32.45s (slow by 4.75s) **TOTAL SP** 117%

This would have had the looks of a run-of-the-mill Princess Royal except for the presence of OUIJA BOARD, and while it was great to see her back in the winner's enclosure, she was fully entitled to win in the style she did. Bookmakers surely overreacted in making her as short as 5-4 (Hills) for a repeat win in the Breeders' Cup Filly & Mare. She was the outstanding middle-distance filly of her generation at three but had been off the track for 101 days since the Prince of Wales's, in which she was injured, and had an interrupted preparation, so she had it all to prove again here. However, she faced nothing good enough to test her properly, because she carried no penalty and had upwards of 14lb in hand according to her BHB mark, and even more on *Racing Post* Ratings. In a race in which the principals all came from the back of the field, she made her ground smoothly on the outside and was committed with more than two furlongs to run, but while she was always in full command thereafter, she was kept up to her work and a bare two-and-a-half-length beating of Briolette (admittedly improving, but a handicap winner off only 92 at Leopardstown on her previous start) does not amount to Group 1 form. If she is back to last year's form when she goes to post for the Breeders' Cup, she will take plenty of beating, but there must be better value in the lists. Interestingly, connections are not entirely ruling out a return to Longchamp for either the Arc or the Opera.

BELMONT PARK

29 October 2005
Yielding

7:35 Emirates Airline Breeders' Cup Filly & Mare Turf (Grade 1) (Fillies & Mares) (Turf) (3yo+) 1m2f

[off 7:40]£287,083.00, £110,417.00, £60,729.00, £31,469.00, £16,563.00

			Draw	TRAINER	Age	Wgt	JOCKEY	SP	OR	TS	RPR
1		Intercontinental (GB)	10	R J Frankel	5	8-11	R Bejarano	14/1	—		120
2	1¼	Ouija Board (GB)	13	E A L Dunlop	4	8-11	J D Bailey	2/1F	—		118
3	nk	Film Maker (USA)	2	H G Motion	5	8-11 b	P Valenzuela	14/1	—		117
4	4	Wonder Again	7	James J Toner	6	8-11	E Prado	11/2	—		110
5	2	Favourable Terms (GB)	9	Sir Michael Stoute	5	8-11	M J Kinane	20/1	—		106
6	1	Wend	5	W Mott	4	8-11	J R Velazquez	14/1	—		104
7	nk	Angara (GB)	14	P L Biancone	4	8-11	Gary Stevens	33/1	—		104
8	4¾	Megahertz (GB)	8	R J Frankel	6	8-11	A Solis	6/1	—		95
9	1½	Karen's Caper	12	J H M Gosden	3	8-7	R Albarado	16/1	—		94
10	2¾	Mona Lisa (GB)	11	A P O'Brien	3	8-7	K Fallon	16/1	—		89
11	¾	Luas Line (IRE)	1	David Wachman	3	8-7	C Soumillon	20/1	—		87
12	5½	Flip Flop (FR)	6	B Cecil	4	8-11	G K Gomez	33/1	—		76
13	7¼	Riskaverse	4	Patrick J Kelly	6	8-11	J Santos	16/1	—		63
14	6¼	Sundrop (JPN)	3	Saeed Bin Suroor	4	8-11	L Dettori	25/1	—		52

14 ran TIME 2m 2.34s **TOTAL SP** 119%

TOKYO

27 November 2005
Firm

6:20 Japan Cup (Group 1) (3yo+) 1m4f

[off 6:20]£1,290,418.00, £513,923.00, £323,042.00, £193,158.00, £127,078.00, £88,954.00

			Draw	TRAINER	Age	Wgt	JOCKEY	SP	OR	TS	RPR
1		Alkaased (USA)	14	L M Cumani	5	8-13	L Dettori	96/10	—		125
2	nse	Heart's Cry	16	K Hashiguchi	4	8-13	C-P Lemaire	62/10	—		125
3	1¾	Zenno Rob Roy	8	Kazuo Fujisawa	5	8-13	K Desormeaux	11/10F	—		122
4	nse	Lincoln	5	H Otonashi	5	8-13	Y Take	195/10	—		122
5	nk	Ouija Board (GB)	6	E A L Dunlop	4	8-9	K Fallon	118/10	—		117
6	1½	Sunrise Pegasus	13	S Ishizaka	7	8-13	H Goto	71/1	—		119
7	½	Heavenly Romance	10	S Yamamoto	5	8-9 b	Mikio Matsunaga	185/10	—		114
8	½	Bago (FR)	12	J E Pease	4	8-13	T Gillet	119/10	—		117
9	nk	Suzuka Mambo	17	M Hashida	4	8-13	K Ando	25/1	—		117
10	1¼	Tap Dance City (USA)	2	S Sasaki	8	8-13	T Sato	162/10	—		115
11	¾	Admire Japan	4	H Matsuda	3	8-9	N Yokoyama	109/10	—		116
12	1¼	Better Talk Now (USA)	7	H G Motion	6	8-13 b	R A Dominguez	33/1	—		112
13	nse	Warrsan (IRE)	3	C E Brittain	7	8-13	Jamie Spencer	96/1	—		112
14	½	Cosmo Bulk (JPN)	11	K Tabe	4	8-13	D Bonilla	49/1	—		111
15	3	My Sole Sound	1	Katsuichi Nishiura	6	8-13	M Honda	137/1	—		106
16	6	King's Drama (IRE)	15	R J Frankel	5	8-13	E Prado	59/1	—		96
17	3½	Big Gold (JPN)	18	T Nakao	7	8-13	R Wada	134/1	—		91
18	¾	Stormy Cafe	9	F Kojima	3	8-9	H Shii	70/1	—		92

18 ran TIME 2m 22.10s **TOTAL SP** 126%

SHA TIN

11 December 2005

Good To Firm

6:10   Cathay Pacific Hong Kong Vase (Group 1) (3yo+) 1m4f

[off 6:11]£536,193.00, £201,072.00, £100,536.00, £53,619.00, £30,161.00, £16,756.00

			Draw	TRAINER	Age	Wgt	JOCKEY	SP	OR	TS	RPR
1		Ouija Board (GB)	7	E A L Dunlop	4	8-10	K Fallon	5/2	—		119+
2	2¾	Six Sense	11	H Nagahama	3	8-9 h	H Shii	33/1	—		119
3	shd	Best Gift (NZ)	8	J Moore	4	9-0	D Whyte	16/1	—		119
4	½	Shamdala (IRE)	4	A De Royer-Dupre	3	9-0	C Soumillon	16/1	—		114
5	½	Westerner (GB)	6	E Lellouche	6	9-0	O Peslier	9/4F	—		117
6	nk	Reefscape (GB)	2	A Fabre	4	9-0	Richard Hughes	16/1	—		117
7	shd	Samando	9	F Doumen	5	8-10	E Legrix	25/1	—		113
8	shd	Sweet Stream (ITY)	3	J E Hammond	5	8-10	T Gillet	9/1	—		113
9	¾	Cherry Mix (FR)	12	Saeed Bin Suroor	4	9-0	L Dettori	8/1	—		115
10	shd	Saturn (IRE)	5	C Fownes	5	9-0 h	R Fradd	40/1	—		115
11	2¼	Norse Dancer (IRE)	1	D R C Elsworth	5	9-0	Martin Dwyer	20/1	—		112
12	7	Warrsan (IRE)	10	C E Brittain	7	9-0	Jamie Spencer	16/1	—		101

12 ran TIME 2m 28.90s   **TOTAL SP** 117%

NAD AL SHEBA

25 March 2006

Good To Firm

3:50   Dubai Sheema Classic (Sponsored by Nakheel) (Group 1) (Turf) (4yo+) 1m4f

[off 3:52]£1,744,186.05, £581,395.35, £290,697.67, £145,348.84, £87,209.30, £58,139.53

			Draw	TRAINER	Age	Wgt	JOCKEY	SP	OR	TS	RPR
1		Heart's Cry (JPN)	13	K Hashiguchi	5	8-11	C-P Lemaire	11/4		102	125+
2	4¼	Collier Hill (GB)	3	G A Swinbank	8	8-11	Dean McKeown	22/1	116	95	117
3	1¼	Falstaff (IRE)	2	M F De Kock	4	8-11 b	J Murtagh	25/1	113	95	117
4	3½	Ouija Board (GB)	8	E A L Dunlop	5	8-7	K Fallon	9/4F		83	106+
5	5¾	Alexander Goldrun (IRE)	7	J S Bolger	5	8-7	K J Manning	10/1	116	74	97+
6	2¼	Alayan (IRE)	12	John M Oxx	4	8-11	M J Kinane	20/1	113	76	100
7	½	Layman (USA)	1	I Mohammed	4	8-11 t	Kerrin McEvoy	50/1	111	75	99
8	¾	Norse Dancer (IRE)	10	D R C Elsworth	6	8-11	John Egan	25/1		72	96
9	3¾	Mustanfar (USA)	5	K McLaughlin	5	8-11 v	R Hills	50/1		66	90
10	½	Punch Punch (BRZ)	6	C Morgado	5	8-11 v	M Almeida	40/1	110	65	89
11	2¾	Oracle West (SAF)	4	M F De Kock	5	8-11	K Shea	12/1	116	61	85
12	2½	Relaxed Gesture (IRE)	14	Christophe Clement	5	8-11 t	C Nakatani	7/1		56	81
13	3¼	Greys Inn (USA)	9	M F De Kock	6	8-11	W C Marwing	15/2	115	51	77
14	dist	Shanty Star (IRE)	11	R Bouresly	6	8-11	G Avranche	66/1	110	—	—

14 ran TIME 2m 31.89s (slow by 1.89s)   **TOTAL SP** 123%

SHA TIN

23 April 2006

Good To Firm

9:30 Audemars Piguet Queen Elizabeth II Cup (Group 1) (3yo+) 1m2f

[off 9:31]£601,052.00, £225,394.00, £112,697.00, £60,105.00, £33,809.00, £18,783.00

			Draw	TRAINER	Age	Wgt	JOCKEY	SP	OR	TS	RPR
1		Irridescence (SAF)	6	M F De Kock	5	8-10	W C Marwing	5/1		—	118
2	hd	Best Gift (NZ)	10	J Moore	5	9-0	E Saint-Martin	12/1		—	121
3	shd	Ouija Board (GB)	8	E A L Dunlop	5	8-10	L Dettori	5/2F		—	117
4	1½	Super Kid (NZ)	2	J Moore	7	9-0	S Dye	9/1		—	118
5	1¾	Bullish Luck (USA)	5	A S Cruz	7	9-0 b	B Prebble	10/1		—	115
6	1¼	Viva Pataca (GB)	12	J Moore	4	9-0	G Mosse	9/2		—	113
7	1¼	Bowman's Crossing (IRE)	3	C Fownes	7	9-0	Dwayne Dunn	22/1		—	111
8	nk	Green Treasure (AUS)	4	D Cruz	5	9-0	Y T Cheng	33/1		—	110
9	1¼	Russian Pearl (NZ)	13	A S Cruz	6	9-0	F Coetzee	14/1		—	108
10	shd	River Dancer (IRE)	7	J Size	7	9-0	G Schofield	66/1		—	108
11	6	Falstaff (IRE)	11	M F De Kock	4	9-0 b	D Whyte	16/1		—	97
12	1½	Laverock (IRE)	1	C Laffon-Parias	4	9-0	M Blancpain	25/1		—	94
13	7¾	Norse Dancer (IRE)	9	D R C Elsworth	6	9-0	Darryll Holland	20/1		—	80

13 ran TIME 2m 2.00s   **TOTAL SP** 120%

EPSOM

02 June 2006

Good

3:25 Vodafone Coronation Cup (Group 1) (Class 1) (4yo+) (1m4f10y) 1m4f

[off 3:29]£141,950.00, £53,800.00, £26,925.00, £13,425.00, £6,725.00, £3,375.00

			Draw	TRAINER	Age	Wgt	JOCKEY	SP	OR	TS	RPR
1		Shirocco (GER)	5	A Fabre	5	9-0	C Soumillon	8/11F		104	124
2	1¾	Ouija Board (GB)	2	E A L Dunlop	5	8-11	L Dettori	11/4	117	98	118
3	½	Enforcer (GB)	3	W R Muir	4	9-0	Martin Dwyer	66/1	109	100	120
4	2½	Ace (IRE)	1	A P O'Brien	5	9-0	K Fallon	11/2		96	116
5	2½	Notable Guest (USA)	6	Sir Michael Stoute	5	9-0	Richard Hughes	14/1	112	92	112
6	9	Something Exciting (GB)	4	D R C Elsworth	4	8-11	T Quinn	50/1	112	74	95

6 ran TIME 2m 37.64s (slow by 1.64s)   **TOTAL SP** 110%

OUIJA BOARD, returning for the first time to the scene of her runaway Oaks win, ran another blinder, and she would have been a shade closer but for being eased near the finish when pursuit was hopeless. A stronger pace would have suited, but that's not to say she would have beaten Shirocco under any circumstances. The Hardwicke and the Prince of Wales's are the options now, and connections do not rule out the former, even though it's a Group 2.

ASCOT

2 June 2006

Good To Firm

3:50   Prince of Wales's Stakes (Group 1) (Class 1) (4yo+) 1m2f

[off 3:50]£211,207.40, £80,049.02, £40,061.71, £19,975.06, £10,006.13, £5,021.66

			Draw	TRAINER	Age	Wgt	JOCKEY	SP	OR	TS	RPR
1		**Ouija Board**	5	E A L Dunlop	5	8-11	O Peslier	8/1	117	100	124+
2	½	**Electrocutionist (USA)**	4	Saeed Bin Suroor	5	9-0	L Dettori	9/4	124	102	125
3	¾	**Manduro (GER)**	6	A Fabre	4	9-0	C Soumillon	12/1		101	124
4	¾	**David Junior (USA)**	3	B J Meehan	4	9-0	Jamie Spencer	11/8F	123	99	122
5	shd	**Notnowcato (GB)**	1	Sir Michael Stoute	4	9-0	M J Kinane	12/1	112	99	122
6	1	**Corre Caminos (FR)**	2	M Delzangles	4	9-0	T Jarnet	33/1		97	120+
7	1¼	**Ace (IRE)**	7	A P O'Brien	5	9-0 v	K Fallon	9/1		95	118

7 ran TIME 2m 6.92s (slow by 1.22s)   **TOTAL SP** 112%

Given that it wasn't run at an end-to-end gallop, many experts will knock the 2006 Prince Of Wales's, but the race was very likely still the platform for the greatest performance yet from the quite wonderful OUIJA BOARD. Settled on the rail in fifth from Swinley Bottom to the straight, she travelled beautifully under Olivier Peslier – not surprising, given the sedate tempo – but still had a few lengths to find on levelling up. Also, she was momentarily checked and had to be brought wide to challenge a furlong and a half out, and as a result was required to accelerate, having lost momentum. However, when she did quicken, she did so in outstanding fashion, mowing down those in front of her until heading Electrocutionist inside the final half-furlong. Once in front, she pulled half a length clear and arguably won a shade cosily. Although perceived wisdom had been that Ouija Board was better over a mile and a half – she had never previously won a Group 1 over ten furlongs – she has never been short of speed. Her final two-furlong split when an unlucky third in Hong Kong in April was exceedingly quick, while to some eyes she was slightly outstayed by Shirocco when second in the Coronation Cup. Even so, it was still a brave call by connections to come here, as carrying a penalty in Saturday's Hardwicke Stakes looked an easier option. However, the Ouija Board team have never been anything but brave, a point proven by the fact she continues to race at five, and their bravery was rewarded. Credit also goes to the choice of Peslier as rider, for the ace French jockey was perfectly suited to the steadily run heat that materialised. Summing up what Ouija Board did here is not easy, but this was indisputably a run that confirmed her to be the complete article, in possession of a blinding turn of foot and a powerful will to win. Her pre-race official rating of 117 insulted her, and this fifth Group 1 victory should rectify that. Given that this was her fourth run of the year, a break is on the cards, although she would have to be a serious contender if supplemented to the King George. Longer term, she will represent Britain again in the Breeders' Cup Filly & Mare Turf and Hong Kong Vase, and, in Ouija Board, Britain will be represented by a horse who can justifiably be called one of the finest mares of the modern era.

SANDOWN

08 July 2006

Good To Firm

3:15 Coral-Eclipse Stakes (Group 1) (Class 1) (3yo+) (1m2f7y) 1m2f

[off 3:16]£260,620.20, £98,776.80, £49,434.30, £24,648.30, £12,347.10, £6,196.50

			Draw	TRAINER	Age	Wgt	JOCKEY	SP	OR	TS	RPR
1		David Junior (USA)	2	B J Meehan	4	9-7	Jamie Spencer	9/4	123	89	122
2	1½	Notnowcato (GB)	6	Sir Michael Stoute	4	9-7	M J Kinane	9/1	113	86	119+
3	nk	Blue Monday	8	R Charlton	5	9-7	Steve Drowne	8/1		86	118
4	shd	Aussie Rules (USA)	3	A P O´Brien	3	8-10	Alan Munro	11/2		86	116
5	2	Ouija Board (GB)	7	E A L Dunlop	5	9-4	C Soumillon	2/1F	117	79	115+
6	1	Snoqualmie Boy (GB)	5	D R C Elsworth	3	8-10	John Egan	22/1		80	111
7	1¾	Royal Alchemist	9	B J Meehan	4	9-4	Michael Tebbutt	100/1	102	74	106
8	¾	Hattan (IRE)	1	C E Brittain	4	9-7	Kerrin McEvoy	66/1	108	75	108
9	7	Notable Guest (USA)	4	Sir Michael Stoute	5	9-7	Richard Hughes	16/1	112	61	94

9 ran TIME 2m 7.31s (slow by 0.31s) **TOTAL SP** 113%

For the third time in five races this year we did not see the best of OUIJA BOARD, who was ridden by her eighth different jockey, and one with precious little experience of the course. Having held Ouija Board up near the back of the field, Soumillon found himself repeatedly boxed in from 2f out, with horses in front of him and Aussie Rules legitimately holding him in on the outside. When an opening came it soon closed again, and at one point approaching the furlong marker she stumbled slightly, although it made no difference as the damage was already done by that stage. Nobody can say for sure where she might have finished had Soumillon elected to produce her towards the outside, but when Ouija Board found herself on David Junior's inside in a tactical race at Royal Ascot she was able to drop back a shade and come around him, then quicken up so well that she beat him by 2l. This time she never had the opportunity to unleash her trademark turn of foot.

GOODWOOD

05 August 2006

Good To Firm

2:30   Vodafone Nassau Stakes (Group 1) (Fillies & Mares) (Class 1) (3yo+) (1m1f192y) 1m2f

[off 2:37]£113,560.00, £43,040.00, £21,540.00, £10,740.00, £5,380.00, £2,700.00

			Draw	TRAINER	Age	Wgt	JOCKEY	SP	OR	TS	RP
1		Ouija Board	7	E A L Dunlop	5	9-5	L Dettori	EvensF	120	104	124
2	shd	Alexander Goldrun (IRE)	5	J S Bolger	5	9-5	K J Manning	9/2		104	123
3	2	Nannina (GB)	4	J H M Gosden	3	8-10	Jimmy Fortune	4/1	117	100	119
4	2½	Chelsea Rose (IRE)	1	C Collins	4	9-5	P Shanahan	12/1		95	115
5	2	Echelon (GB)	3	Sir Michael Stoute	4	9-5	K Darley	16/1	107	92	111
6	1½	Race For The Stars (USA)	2	A P O'Brien	3	8-10	M J Kinane	10/1		89	108
7	5	Nasheej (USA)	6	R Hannon	3	8-10	Ryan Moore	20/1	111	79	99

7 ran TIME 2m 4.47s (fast by 0.53s)   **TOTAL SP** 115%

This looked an exceptionally strong renewal on paper with the winners of 13 Group 1 races on show. Not one of the seven runners was rated less than 110, while the contest provided an intriguing clash of the generations with a trio of three-year-olds – including the Coronation Stakes and Fillies' Mile winner – taking on a quartet of older horses that included two of the very best racemares of recent years. In short, it looked a cracker, with the only worry beforehand being the possible absence of early pace. However, that fear was not borne out after Chelsea Rose set a respectable gallop, followed just behind by OUIJA BOARD, ridden much more prominently than on occasions in the past and considerably more so than in the nightmare that was the Eclipse. Sent to the front three furlongs out by Frankie Dettori, who was keen for his mount not to be outspeeded by the specialist milers, Ouija Board was almost immediately joined by Alexander Goldrun and for well over two furlongs the two five-year-olds engaged in a stirring tussle that seemed to be edging the way of Alexander Goldrun until Ouija Board got her head back in front in the final stride. Both mares emerged from the fight with the utmost credit. Almost every superlative has already been heaped upon Ouija Board – deservedly so – and she is worthy of them being repeated after this her sixth top-flight triumph. It is impossible to say what would have happened had she not been so horribly and repeatedly hampered in the Eclipse, but she went to Sandown on the highest of highs after defeating Electrocutionist and the subsequent Sandown victor David Junior at Royal Ascot. Previously second to Shirocco in the Coronation Cup after another unlucky defeat in Hong Kong and an earlier troubled trip around Nad Al Sheba, she underlined here both her toughness and durability. While Dettori's ride was exemplary, he was also obliged to ride Ouija Board in a way that probably did not suit her, as she likes to have a target at which to aim. Nevertheless, she overcame that to score and, while this may not rank as her very best performance judged on a literal interpretation of the form, it comes pretty close given that the 117-rated Nannina was a tad over two lengths back in third. Her own wellbeing has continually delayed her mid-season break, but she surely deserves that break now prior to an autumn campaign that will no doubt revolve primarily around a bid to win back her Breeders' Cup crown. The most popular Flat racehorse in Britain by some way, she is one of the finest racemares we have seen and her connections should once again be applauded for campaigning her so enthusiastically.

LEOPARDSTOWN

09 September 2006

Good To Firm

3:55   Baileys Irish Champion Stakes (Group 1) (3yo+) 1m2f

[off 3:55]£426,896.55, £130,344.83, £61,379.31, £20,000.00, £13,103.45

			Draw	TRAINER	Age	Wgt	JOCKEY	SP	OR	TS	RPR
1		Dylan Thomas	2	A P O'Brien	3	9-0	K Fallon	13/8F	124	114	127
2	nk	Ouija Board (GB)	5	E A L Dunlop	5	9-4	Jamie Spencer	11/4		110	124
3	2½	Alexander Goldrun (IRE)	3	J S Bolger	5	9-4	K J Manning	3/1	120	105	119
4	1½	Mustameet (USA)	6	Kevin Prendergast	5	9-7	D P McDonogh	8/1	117	106	119
5	2½	Ace	4	A P O'Brien	5	9-7	M J Kinane	12/1	114	101	114

5 ran TIME 2m 2.90s (fast by 2.60s) **TOTAL SP** 108%

OUIJA BOARD, despite her many remarkable feats, has also been involved in more than her fair share of scrapes. Ironically, on this occasion the race could hardly have developed more smoothly for her, and yet ultimately that actually managed to conspire against her. The mare travelled really strongly into the straight, at which point her rider's main concern was to establish where he was positioned relative to his great rival from the Nassau Stakes, Alexander Goldrun. With the runners fanning out and no danger of traffic problems, Ouija Board was committed fully a furlong and a half out, taking over after the winner had briefly hit the front. The result of her move was that Dylan Thomas had enough time to build a counter-attack on the inside in the last furlong, a circumstance that would not have been likely to arise had Ouija Board's challenge been delayed.

CHURCHILL DOWNS

04 November 2006

Firm

6:55   Emirates Airline Breeders' Cup Filly & Mare Turf (Grade 1) (3yo+) 1m3f

[off 6:56]£690,698.00, £255,814.00, £127,907.00, £65,233.00, £31,977.00

			Draw	TRAINER	Age	Wgt	JOCKEY	SP	OR	TS	RPR
1		Ouija Board (GB)	2	E A L Dunlop	5	8-11	L Dettori	6/4F	—		123
2	2¼	Film Maker (USA)	4	H G Motion	6	8-11 b	E Prado	10/1	—		119
3	nk	Honey Ryder	5	T Pletcher	5	8-11 b	J R Velazquez	8/1	—		119
4	1¾	Wait A While (USA)	7	T Pletcher	3	8-7	G K Gomez	5/2	—		117
5	1	Satwa Queen (FR)	9	J De Roualle	4	8-11	T Thulliez	7/1	—		114
6	nk	My Typhoon (IRE)	8	W Mott	4	8-11	R Albarado	33/1	—		114
7	4½	Mauralakana (FR)	3	P L Biancone	3	8-7	J R Leparoux	20/1	—		107
8	2¼	Dancing Edie	1	Craig Dollase	4	8-11	C Nakatani	40/1	—		103
9	6½	Quiet Royal	6	T Pletcher	3	8-7	O Peslier	33/1	—		93
10	12¾	Germance	10	J-C Rouget	3	8-7	C Soumillon	16/1	—		73

10 ran TIME 2m 14.55s **TOTAL SP** 120%

OUIJA BOARD cemented her claims to be accorded a position within the pantheon of great race mares with an emotional success under an assured Frankie Dettori. Moving off the inside to keep tabs on second favourite Wait A While, she unleashed her characteristic acceleration to overwhelm the opposition, racing down the middle of the turf track which was the place to be all day. In repeating her success at Lone Star in 2004, Ouija Board became only the seventh horse to win two Breeders' Cup races. And had Jerry Bailey not given her too much to do in last season's renewal, she would surely have made it three. Connections are planning one or two more races in the Far East before she retires to the paddocks, though there is really nothing more she needs to achieve. As well as a variety of Europe's top jockeys, she has arguably carried British Flat racing on her back during an era in which there have been few other home-trained superstars to get excited about.

TOKYO

26 November 2006

Firm

6:20 **Japan Cup (Grade 1) (3yo+)** 1m4f

[off 0:00]£1,233,776.00, £493,510.00, £310,912.00, £187,534.00, £123,378.00

			Draw	TRAINER	Age	Wgt	JOCKEY	SP	OR	TS	RPR
1		Deep Impact	6	Y Ikee	4	9-0	Y Take	30/100F		—	127+
2	2	Dream Passport	7	H Matsuda	3	8-9	Y Iwata	152/10		—	124
3	½	Ouija Board (GB)	3	E A L Dunlop	5	8-9	L Dettori	17/2		—	117
4	1	Cosmo Bulk	10	K Tabe	5	9-0	F Igarashi	40/1		—	121
5	1½	Fusaichi Pandora	8	T Shirai	3	8-5	Y Fukunaga	52/1		—	116
6	nse	Meisho Samson	11	T Setoguchi	3	8-9	M Ishibashi	15/1		—	119
7	½	Freedonia (GB)	9	J E Hammond	4	8-9	T Gillet	89/1		—	113
8	¾	Swift Current (JPN)	2	Hideyuki Mori	5	9-0	N Yokoyama	42/1		—	117
9	3½	Tosen Shana O	5	Hideyuki Mori	3	8-9	H Goto	150/1		—	112
10	6	Heart's Cry	1	K Hashiguchi	5	9-0	C-P Lemaire	58/10		—	102
11	3½	Yukino Sun Royal	4	S Masuzawa	9	9-0	Katsuharu Tanaka	216/1		—	97

11 ran TIME 2m 25.10s **TOTAL SP** 123%

The 2006 Japan Cup proved the end of a glorious racing career of which we could only have dreamt when the foaling record of Selection Board's 2001 foal was filled in at Stanley House Stud!

204

ACKNOWLEDGEMENTS

Just as the Ouija Board story has been a major team effort, so has the publication of this book.

When I set off down the route of trying to write the Ouija Board story, I had no idea how time-consuming and difficult it would prove, and without Sean Magee it would never have happened at all. He and I have spent countless hours together working through the mass of material which I and others have accumulated, and his skill has crafted my words into a readable shape.

We have had a lot of fun reliving the story through the nine large volumes of press cuttings that Ouija Board has generated, and we would never have had this material assembled without the efforts of Liz Cowdy and Andrea Poole.

Much of the collaboration between Sean and myself took place at the offices of Fleming Family and Partners in London, where Sue Kilcoyne helped the project in many different ways.

At Gainsborough Stables I am especially grateful to Ed and Becky Dunlop, Chris Hinson, Steve Young, Robin Trevor-Jones, Pat Evens and Angela Lowe for sharing their memories and reminding me of the bits I had forgotten or never knew, while at Stanley House Stud I was helped in the same way by my brother Peter Stanley, Pat Cronin and Nancy Pollitt. Eugene and Jane Stanford shared their reminiscences of breaking Ouija Board in.

At Highdown, Jonathan Taylor and Julian Brown steered the book towards publication, while Adrian Morrish has produced a volume with a design quality worthy of its subject.

I am also very grateful to my old prep school friend Henry Birtles for allowing me to reproduce his wonderful poem about Ouija Board.

Closer to home, my darling wife Cazzy's input has been invaluable in reminding me when my memory was found lacking, and reading and commenting on many different proofs.

And finally, thanks to Brough Scott. Having had the idea of writing this book, I had no idea how to execute it, but all that changed as I walked around Royal Liverpool Golf Club at the 2006 Open, following the Tiger Woods match. Kneeling on the ground so that I did not obscure any views as Tiger lined up a shot, I found myself next to Brough, who was following the match for the *Sunday Telegraph*. 'Highdown are thinking about producing a book on Ouija Board,' he told me. 'So am I!', I replied – and that was when the idea started to become a reality …

D.

ILLUSTRATIONS

All photographs in this book are copyright the *Racing Post*, with the following exceptions:

Lord Derby: pages 45, 51, 53, 56, 60, 67, 78, 94, 95, 101, 106, 109, 112 (lower), 114, 121, 122, 140, 156, 166, 167, 172, 176, 179; The Derby Collection 10, 14, 182; Arnhel de Serra 12, 92-3; Arlington Park 17; Stanley House Stud 21, 24; George Selwyn 77, 125, 170-1; Action Images 136; Osborne Studio Gallery 144; Goodwood Racecourse 145; Lane's End Farm 180-1.

The map on pages 188-189 is by John Schwartz.